Astrology on the Job

WHAT THE STARS AND PLANETS CAN TELL YOU ABOUT:

✿ Bosses, coworkers, employees, and competitors ✿ How sun and moon signs affect communication ✿ Sailing through conflict with coworkers ✿ Making the most of career opportunities

CAROLYN REYNOLDS

Contemporary Books

*Chicago   New York   San Francisco   Lisbon   London   Madrid   Mexico City
Milan   New Delhi   San Juan   Seoul   Singapore   Sydney   Toronto*

Library of Congress Cataloging-in-Publication Data

Reynolds, Carolyn.
     Astrology on the job / Carolyn Reynolds.
        p.   cm.
     Includes index.
     ISBN 0-7373-0552-5
     1. Astrology and business.   2. Success in business—Miscellanea.
3. Interpersonal relations—Miscellanea.   I. Title.

    BF1729.B8 R46   2001
    133.5—dc21   00-066003

Contemporary Books

A Division of The **McGraw·Hill** *Companies*

1 2 3 4 5 6 7 8 9 0 DOH/DOH 0 9 8 7 6 5 4 3 2 1

ISBN 0-7373-0552-5

This book was set in Book Antiqua
Printed and bound by R. R. Donnelley

Cover design by Laurie Young
Cover art by Jui Ishida
Interior design by Linda M. Robertson, Michael Bass Associates

McGraw-Hill books are available at special quantity discounts to use as premiums and sales promotions, or for use in corporate training programs. For more information, please write to the Director of Special Sales, Professional Publishing, McGraw-Hill, Two Penn Plaza, New York, NY 10121-2298. Or contact your local bookstore.

Throughout the book, for simplicity and brevity, the author has used the personal pronouns *he*, *his*, *him*, and *himself* to refer to both males and females.

This book is printed on acid-free paper.

First, for now and always, to my beloved mother, who has gone on to a higher plane. And to my wonderful husband, Patrick, who is my shining star in broad daylight, my best friend, and my former boss. Finally, to Stevie, our Wheaten Terrier, who sat with me during the writing of this book and interrupted my schedule with his own career needs and television shoots. At our house everybody has a job.

CONTENTS

℃

Contents

ACKNOWLEDGMENTS

One night agent extraordinaire Sagittarius Jeff Herman had an idea for this book. It woke him from an East Coast sleep. Meanwhile on the West Coast, with perfect Capricorn timing, I sent him a proposal. The proposal ultimately landed on the desk of my adorable, enthusiastic, coffee-cup-holding senior editor, Hudson Perigo, also a Sagittarius. Along the way, executive editor Peter Hoffman, a wonderful Virgo, assisted with the manuscript. This book then, like all projects, was a team effort. I thank my coworkers.

PART ONE

INTRODUCTION OF
THE FIRST SIX SIGNS

Do you require a specific agenda to accomplish your tasks in work and life? Or do you find that you work best in a more free-flowing work style? Do you work long hours but find you can't get to meetings on time? Do you put off a new project until the last possible minute or start working on it as soon as you learn about it? Perhaps you work the way you do because of the astrological significance of the day of your birth.

Would you like to know more about working effectively with people who are different from you? Now you can learn to read people through astrological clues to character and temperament. Discover the hidden needs in people that apply to business and everyday living.

Astrology on the Job makes it easy for you to uncover your own work type and the working styles of your coworkers and business associates. Take a new look at your office through astrology and zodiac type watching to observe the different kinds of intelligence and the combinations of learning styles.

What is astrology, and can it be that the date of our birth is the common denominator of work styles?

Astrology, much more than the forecast we read in the newspapers each day, has been used for years to predict the best times for farmers to plant and harvest. Before that, the phases of the moon were used for primitive man to select the best times to hunt and fish. They kept track of the moon phases with notches on reindeer horns.

Life has seasons and cycles. While we all know and recognize this, some of us have used this for the timing of events and the prediction of possibilities.

There is correlation between the effects of sunlight on plants and individuals. Winter is different from summer, just as winter-born individuals are different from the summer-born.

After years of myth, we now have the scientific equipment to register solar flares and can demonstrate that the flares do affect conditions here on earth. Like other living organisms, we are encouraged or discouraged in growth by the sun.

The fables of the moon, the moon lore of centuries, can now be documented. We have more crime during a full moon. Doctors experience patients bleeding more during surgery scheduled during the full moon. Fact is, we do respond to the motions of the heavens, and we have since the day of our birth.

The day of your birth is related to astrology by the placement of the sun in the horizons at the time of your arrival here on earth; hence your astrological sun sign. Like any other imprint by sunlight and moonlight, your personality can be illuminated by the two luminaries.

Many theories exist about business aptitudes, successes, and career interests. Is your work style concrete or abstract? What type of intelligence do you possess? Are you musical and mathematical like the Taurus or interpersonal like the Pisces?

The way we work tells as much as why we work or where we work. Whether you are an artistically, mechanically, or physically inclined worker, everyone approaches his tasks differently.

In my work as a job placement counselor and in preparation for this book, I have taken and administered dozens of vocational tests and interviewed hundreds of employers from both small and large companies. I noticed the rate of success at work was more often linked to personality traits than aptitude tests.

This made me curious, and I wondered if the day of an individual's birth could provide clues to work habits, inclinations, and motivation. As a professional astrologer, I naturally made the leap that perhaps these characteristics were rooted in our sun signs.

Can your astrological sign predispose you to certain work traits? I believe it can and does.

This book combines vocational typology, which says there is a correlation between personality type and learning style in the workplace, with the twelve astrological types at birth. In this day of changing technology, E-business, teleconferencing, and the Internet, we need an update on career choices. As the world allows for more entrepreneurial work options, we all need fresh new insights in what is truly the Age of Aquarius.

Astrology on the Job is a timely book for those of us wanting better relationships at work, more effective products and services, and a leg up in the rise to the top.

Here is my gift to you, my fellow worker: a guide to understanding the way we work and the best way for all of us to work together.

Ultimately, we will all get to the top of our own charts. We will get there through the grace of the Libra, the luck of the Sagittarius, the determination of the Capricorn. And, we will get there sooner if we allow others to express themselves, warts and all. In my case, it's a messy, littered, and book-strewn office where I work happily in utter chaos.

A FEW BASIC ASTROLOGICAL TERMS

Over eons of observation, astrologers have noted that certain personality traits or characteristics fall into the four elements of fire, earth, air, and water. Most of us have heard expressions such as, she's got fire in her veins, he's the salt of the earth, his head is in the clouds, or still waters run deep. Actually, the fire signs of Aries, Leo, and Sagittarius *do* have fire in their veins—they like action and excitement, and this makes them spontaneous and creative. Meanwhile, the earth signs of Taurus, Virgo, and Capricorn are down-to-earth, practical, hardworking, and often plodding. They approach life and work with a plan, a purpose, and determination. The air signs are the thinkers. Gemini, Libra, and Aquarius weigh outcomes, ponder solutions, and often seem to have their heads in the clouds. They are usually intelligent and idealistic. Finally, we have the water signs of Cancer, Scorpio, and Pisces. These signs are the still waters of the zodiac. They are intuitive, receptive, and able to see things at the core level.

Our modes of expression are also of astrological consideration, and these have been defined as cardinal, fixed, and mutable. The cardinal signs are Aries, Cancer, Libra, and Capricorn. Individuals born under these sun signs are the initiators of our universe—the powerful ones. They like situations in which they can gain control. The fixed signs of Taurus, Leo, Scorpio, and Aquarius move a little more slowly, often resisting changes unless modifications origi-nate with them. Finally, the mutable signs of Gemini, Pisces, Virgo, and Sagittarius are more restless with their energies. They think out of the box, and when this energy is applied at work, they create change, rewrite job descriptions, and move desks around. Often, they seek change for the sheer distraction of it.

How do these energies intermingle? In the following chapters, I will present some strengths of pairings such as that of fire and earth (Wow! What a team!), as well as other pairings that require the participants to be more tolerant of one another. The impor-tant thing to remember is that when we recognize and allow for another's point of view or personality style, we become wonderfully creative and productive. Let's begin our journey by illustrating a typical office setting and all the wondrous players on the stage.

THE OFFICE PLAYERS

Neat Nick comes to the staff meeting with his presentation and notes in order. He has a well thought-out plan and knows he will be able to demonstrate it. The first to arrive, Nick notices his coworkers with amusement as they seat themselves around the conference table. He smoothes his pristine shirt that he's ironed twice.

Kay, hardworking and stable, is the second to arrive. Kay would never make supervisor, or so it seems. She has cookie crumbs on her folders, and she will want to focus on the facts, again. The same old charts and figures she's dwelled on for the past three months. Nick can't understand Kay's nearsighted organizational vision.

The queen, dressed in reds and oranges like the sun, arrives next. Nick wonders what imaginative, off-the-top-of-her-red-head, last-minute brainstorm she would conjure up today. It would be good, no doubt. Is the queen just lucky or what? She's the star all right, yet Nick resents her for her casual approach to her career. Why is it, Nick wonders, that management is always quick to notice the queen?

MaryAnn arrives. She's the conduit that holds the group together. Nurturing and intuitive, she knows the agenda and never needs notes. Notes are superfluous. When things get stirred up, MaryAnn will be the calming voice of the four. Nick works well with MaryAnn, but management doesn't seem to appreciate her, and this baffles him.

The manager is still outside, networking her way through the halls and chatting with everyone. She's always a little too spontaneous for Nick, who thinks she should be setting a good example by being on time. Even though she's popular and verbal, Nick wonders how she has succeeded. He can't imagine why such strong verbal and people skills would be pluses in this organization.

In every office in every part of the world, the four elements and the twelve signs combine to put out fires, deliver newspapers, collect taxes, and teach our children. Whether the industry is service or entertainment, protective or instructive, teams are assembled and coworkers get along.

Sometimes friction, misplaced loyalties, favorable mentoring, and profitable alliances occur within the teams. Sometimes a confusing mix of energies results. But, at all times, an astrological predisposition exists.

So we begin with the twelve astrological types and their work styles.

Few of us are 100 percent anything. For this reason, you may possess most of your sun sign traits, but not all. You may, for example, be an Aries sun sign with other planets (i.e., the moon, Mercury, or even the ascendant) in Taurus. Some of you will find the sign next to your sun sign may factor in or be more applicable to you.

On any given day, each of the planets in our solar system, and the sun and moon, which are luminaries, fall in a zodiac sign. You may be a Scorpio but have the moon, Mercury, and Jupiter in Libra. When a preponderance of planets are in another sign, the person acts more like a Libra, for example, than a Scorpio. Although unusual, this will apply to some.

In my case, I am strongly Capricorn, but my office is a Sagittarian disaster. I work best when I express both energies.

So if you find yourself a curious blend, you are the norm not the exception.

CHAPTER 1

THE INITIATOR

ARIES ■ MARCH 21 TO APRIL 20

HOW TO SPOT AN ARIES

Motivating Υ *Inventive* Υ *Enthusiastic*

Aries usually has straight posture. He walks with confidence, which is reflected in his movements. The Aries' approach to life is like a head-on collision. He has a fast, firm handshake. He usually knocks something over within the first few minutes of meeting you.

Aries is the first to throw out directions, personnel guidelines, and notes in his mad-dash approach to life. He is always in a hurry, which often backfires. Rushing about as he does, fiery Aries often misplaces things, trips over briefcases, and creates havoc as well as excitement.

Some of Aries' most notable characteristics are that he doesn't want to think things over or weigh the consequences. Aries always looks for the chance to lead and initiate action. He often makes instant assessments that turn out to be correct and insightful while seemingly acting on impulse alone. Aries has a fiery temper, and like a match to straw, he is fast to ignite. But, Aries does not usually hold grudges. All this enthusiasm and impetus is compelling to others.

Aries often ends up in an inventive, pioneering field and eventually rises to a position of leadership and authority. Just as Aries leads the zodiac, he often leads the rest of us in life.

Aries has been forging the way since the beginning of time. He was undoubtedly the first of the clan to make fire, organize athletic events, and give seminars on motivation and conquering fear. The natural head of any group, he often goes into business for himself. Some fields in which the Aries excels are: sports professionals (race car driving to ring physicians), career military, pilots, machinists, dentists, miners, and mayors.

WHAT DRIVES THE ARIES?

Adrenaline ϒ *Expression*

Adrenaline rushes fuel the Aries. The sheer expression of the physical is Aries' primary desire. He didn't invent the first airplane to impress his boss. Aries always does what he does for himself.

The slow, plodding movements of the earth signs provoke the Aries. Yet, it is this stop-and-ponder, think-it-through attitude of earth that gets the job done for Aries.

The all-show-no-go attitude of the air signs leaves Aries baffled. Gemini, Libra, and Aquarius often analyze something first, but action-prone Aries takes awhile to adapt to that type of work style.

Fire signs like himself encourage the Aries vision and bring out the "anything you can do I can do better" energies. The dramatic and grand-scale thinking of Orville Wright, a Leo, helped his brother Wilbur with his equally enthusiastic ideas to get the plane off the ground.

Water signs such as Cancer, Scorpio, and Pisces seem to dash Aries' hopes a bit by reminding him that feelings are involved when working with others. Yet, Aries has a big heart and when reminded of things beyond the immediate, he works well with the input of the intuitive water signs.

THE ARIES WORK STYLE

Diverse Duties Υ *Feeling He Makes a Difference*
Challenges Υ *Working at a Fast Pace*

Surprisingly, Aries wants an ordered, uncluttered office. He doesn't like to display his work all over the desks, chairs, walls, and floors. Aries often accessorizes with lots of chrome or metal, a piece of exercise equipment, or weights.

Aries wants floods of new assignments and challenges. He doesn't want a lot of restrictions. Aries craves diverse duties. He prefers fast-paced assignments and something that holds the promise of closure, funding, or resolution. He wants to feel that he has made a difference at the end of the day. Tasks that drag on for months, appear meaningless, or seem unconnected to the end result stress the Aries-born.

THE ARIES STRENGTHS

Physical Intelligence Υ *Will Make a Stand* Υ *Initiates Action*

While many different kinds of intelligence exist, each astrological sign possesses one or more areas in which individuals are most likely to excel. The Aries has a strong constitution and functions best at a physical level. Because of this, Aries has a strong physical IQ. He is able to adapt to circumstances and provide leadership for others who tend to feel more comfortable in following.

Aries is the first to yell "Fire!" to ring bells, start trends, and take action. Aries is loud, bright, strong, and fearless. Aries is the one to take a chance, make a stand, blow up the chemistry lab (a miscalculation, of course). Yes, Aries is accident-prone. Aries is rash. It is, however, this tornado-driven approach to life, the careless abandon and sheer thrill-seeking manner, that fuels the Aries-born.

THE ARIES FAVORITE
WORK ENVIRONMENT

Arenas That Offer Excitement Υ *Stimulating Environments*

Aries loves the outdoors or arenas. He is found in football stands, boxing rings, forest ranger lookouts, arctic and space stations. Brought down to a Main Street address, the Aries workstation may look like others at a casual glance. But, upon closer inspection, you see the photos of his last ski trip, his climb up Everest, or a schedule of upcoming boxing events. Clues are everywhere. When not confined to a desk (ball and chain), you will find Aries in high-pressure environments. It's the bell thing again. He likes the clamor of the day-trading scene and finds the noise and confusion alluring. The clang clang of fire engine sirens rushing to accidents sends endorphins to his brain.

THE ARIES EMPLOYEE/COWORKER

Courageous Υ *Quick-Tempered* Υ *Energetic* Υ *Unstoppable*

Aries is fun, lively, and full of tales of weekends well spent and vacations lived to the fullest. The Aries will never slip into the "I just stayed home and sorted out the paperbacks from the hard covers" or "I finally found the missing socks and got them all matched up." Oh no, not Aries who dreams of swimming with the sharks, not in the office but in Shark Alley off the coast of South Africa. The Aries thinks that the more routine the workweek is, the more extreme the weekend needs to be.

An Aries' cure for a morale problem is a two-hour lunch to include some form of exercise. Aries can experience an occasional bout of depression. Faced with a dismal spell, the Aries is jumping into the cold pool waters at midnight, giving himself pep talks about snapping out of it. He may even slap his own face. Whatever it takes to rid himself of the momentary loss of self-confidence, the Aries will do.

Aries' fierce drive and will inspires and leads his coworkers. He will fight fire-breathing dragon supervisors for you if he believes in you or your project. Forced by management to take his agency ads somewhere else if he can't have the account executive he wants, he will calmly leave the bargaining table and say, "OK then. It's been nice working with you." A natural poker player, Aries is cool and deliberate. He knows he will win. Someone will have to back down, and it won't be him. His confidence sends shock waves. He is determined and unstoppable and the person you need in your corner, ring, or arena.

Another example of the Aries at the negotiating table is a certain famous and multimillion-copy bestselling author. She liked to make up words every now and then, and once, when her editor asked her to change one of her word creations, she refused. Production schedules were in the balance; jobs were in jeopardy. Still, she said, "No."

Production came to a halt; meetings were held and reheld. Unperturbed, she took off to pick some wild berries or climb a mountain.

The publisher, hearing the news of the editor's insistence and the author's refusal, sent red roses to the author with a note that read something like this: "You keep your word. My apologies." Such is the power of Aries' will.

Aries is exciting and fun. Energetic, he is a jolt of caffeine. He likes to come up with new ideas and to help you develop yours. However, don't ever try to take credit for something an Aries has done. Oh no, don't do that.

An Aries worker can be a bit terrifying from time to time, no matter how nice. And Aries is nice and really wants to be your friend. He wants to, I swear he does. It is just that he is temperamental. He is driven and knows no bounds. He doesn't understand the negative, the fearful, the lazy, or the uninspired.

When Aries gets angry, he ignites like emergency flares. He creates chaos and panic in the uninitiated. And, he does so with a loving heart for the most part. After the ashes and soot settle, you find a forgiving friend. Maybe even contrite, if you play your poker hand well.

The generous Aries is usually an easy touch for anyone who is down and out. He likes to share his good fortune, perhaps throw a party after the promotion was a success. Well, heck, there is a party at his place every now and then anyway, for Aries loves a good time and doesn't want to spend his day somber and foreboding in his pinstripes. He doesn't want you to be too serious, either. In fact, Aries views all work and no play to be as disturbing as a near-death experience.

Aries is not a workaholic, and work is only a part of his day. Sixteen other hours a day remain for him to play like the child he is. He wants everyone to leave the building and do something to relax. He will enjoy some action-packed activities until it is time for rest and recharging. He will rest well until the buzzer or alarm goes off. Then he's refueled like a rocket and ready to launch another day.

THE ARIES LEARNING STYLE

Is Impulsive Υ *Is Here-and-Now Oriented*
Needs Physical Demonstration

Anthony Gregorc developed a theory regarding the different ways we each prefer to learn and called it the Gregorc Models of Learning Styles. In his paradigm, individuals prefer learning styles that are concrete, sequential, physical, or random. The way an Aries learns or the way in which his mind works is considered concrete when viewed in this context.

Everyone and every sign observe the same sights and sounds, yet each perceives them in different ways. While at some level we all see what we want to see, we convert information in two distinct fashions. One perceptual quality is the concrete style of learning.

When we think or perceive in a concrete way, we register the world around us via the five senses: touch, sight, smell, taste, and hearing. The sixth sense is considered to be intuitive. Aries only deals with the five senses. But, if he were to have a sixth sense, it would not be of an esoteric nature; it would be vocal or speech. Aries loves to speak things into existence. He wants to see evidence of what he is dealing with in a physical way.

For example, Aries needs to hear the situation first. He doesn't want to have to read between the lines or read your mind. He doesn't want to search for deeper meanings or the obscure. He wants here and now. Remember, *now* is a big word for the Aries. He wants the obvious. He wants it immediately. He wants information presented clearly and concisely. Don't present data with any degree of coyness. Save the hidden agenda for someone else.

While all of us process information from both a concrete and an abstract viewpoint, we have a preference. This preference is where we are most comfortable in learning and working situations.

13

Aries won't pick up on subtlety. Spell it out. If you want to sell him donuts, let him use his senses. He will view them, smell them, and notice the touch as well as the taste. Then he will be ready to hear your sales presentation.

The second component to learning is how we order our information. The Aries prefers unstructured, quick methods of organizing, called random style of learning. This inclines the Aries to learn better when he is given a chance to become curious or the opportunity to be creative and innovative. He wants to work from impulse and natural instinct. He is adventurous in his ordering of information. Whatever your working relationship with the Aries, remember these needs are part of his work style. Don't sell him donuts with the lid closed. This will save both of you frustration and disappointments.

THE BEST WAY FOR AN ARIES TO LEARN

Projects Have Deadlines ⋎ *He Feels in Control*
He Is Not Overwhelmed with Details

Aries prefers to solve problems as they come up. Aries also likes to be creative and entrepreneurial in his projects and assignments. He likes spontaneity in his environment. For him, burnout occurs when he knows what is going to happen at the office from day to day with no surprises.

Aries prefers a fast-paced schedule and isn't afraid to make changes in his office, his duties, or your expectations. He rises to challenges. He doesn't like projects that expand to infinity. He needs boundaries on time, not the how-to.

The Aries understands risk taking, from E-trading to mountain climbing. Since his intelligence is related to the physical, he needs to do more than take your word for things. He needs to try to do what you are telling him to do. Mimicking a task reinforces his learning ability.

Aries is naturally hands-on. Once he has mastered a skill or project, he wants to move on to other challenges. Boredom is Aries' downfall. If he gets bored, he becomes discontented or mischievous. Aries would rather create an incident than have an uneventful week. This is why many times the Aries will burn bridges before even crossing them.

Aries wants to stay in control of his life; therefore, too much structuring, too many rules, or reading detailed office memos seems an intrusion. Tell Aries what he needs to do, not how to do it. Remember, he is not the best team player, and impulsiveness may be his flaw. Remember, too, in working with the Aries that he can be as exceptional as he thinks he is.

THE ARIES INTELLIGENCE

Physical Ƴ *Athletic*

Howard Gardner, a well-known Harvard professor and prominent researcher, has developed the theory that many different kinds of intelligence exist. He has identified seven, while others are speculative.

Recently, emotional intelligence (EIQ) has been suggested as another form of IQ. Daniel Goleman's work on this has opened our eyes in the West to the possibility of genius beyond more traditional measures. The importance of the varieties of mental capacities, or ways to be smart, may really reflect the passions that incline us toward our work.

The Aries type of intelligence, physical intelligence, is an athletic form of intelligence just as valuable as the more intellectual forms of IQ measurements. The Aries demonstrates how his here-and-now approach, physical strengths, and fearless nature are valuable in processing information and getting through life.

Physical energies may also be considered in what shapes Aries' success at work. Aries' high level of energy requires a fine blend of physical and mental strategies. This skill enables him to be inventive and agile with his hands. These strengths open the doors for careers involving mechanical skills. Of course, the Aries learns best by being involved in a physical activity while doing something that is being learned or taught. When he is stuck in an office, Aries finds ways to get out or get around, or at the very least taps fidgeting fingers on the desk. Since Aries requires a physical activity to help him learn and accomplish, this should always be an option. Give Aries room and space in which to work.

When preparing training sessions for the Aries, plan presentations that involve frequent breaks and require only short periods of intense mental concentration. Provide for changes in work duties and environments. Be relaxed with Aries. He's wound up enough. Don't breathe down his neck.

If you want to work with or for an Aries, remember he has a concrete/random, physical learning style. Aries is also of the fire element and the cardinal mode astrologically. A cardinal type is inclined to be more enterprising than other signs; a cardinal personality is one that is most able to overcome difficulties.

The Aries profile includes his need to break down barriers and find positive new ways to do the established, and to lead others by his ability to initiate and speak potentials into action.

Aries, the first of the fire signs, generates more intense reactions than almost any sign of the zodiac. This means that he is a predominately extroverted Myers-Briggs vocational type. The Aries is certain only of the moment, the now. He does not deal well with long-range planning. He is not interested in details and sees the forest rather than the trees.

The Aries does well in careers that react to emergencies. He is great as a troubleshooter and problem solver where time is of the essence. It is the Aries character that defuses the ticking bomb in action movies.

Aries is rarely worried about time in his own life, however. He is often late and believes that an event doesn't start until he arrives. This view of time is one of Aries' most noticeable idiosyncrasies.

Aries likes to figure how things work out of curiosity and for the fun of it. He is not interested in the mechanics or the data in a fact-finding fashion. However, Aries is interested in leading the way to the mission, to the dig, or to the heights or depths of any project.

Aries talks just as quickly as he moves. Because of this, he does not receive instructions well that are dry, humorless, or redundant in any way.

An Aries is quick to be annoyed with long-winded explanations and by now is probably anxious reading this, for example. "Enough already," he thinks. "I want to hear about another sun sign."

Remember, Aries is the first to throw out recipes, instructions, or manuals.

THE ARIES PROFILE

Fire-Breathing Υ *Energetic*

Aries expends energy in every facet of his life and work. He goes to extremes and appears to be driven to overextend or exert himself. Frenzies, conniption fits (as my assistant likes to say), and fire-breathing attacks are the Aries' modus operandi for creating inspired work.

When a fire sign like Aries works with Leo or Sagittarius, you find an astrological working predisposition that emphasizes the fiery, temperamental, and impulsive nature of the elements. In the spice of life, it is two red-hot chilies in the sauce. They can create, illustrate, and promote in every minute of the day.

If you know your ascendant or the ascendant of a coworker and you are an Aries ascendant, you might read the Aries profile for more information on the way he works.

Christine Filiberto, for example, has an Aries ascendant and is the first female amateur boxing referee in the United States as well as the first female international boxing referee in the United States. While Christine could have been a banner-carrying beauty parading around the ring, she chose the challenge. It's the Aries' need to be first and break down barriers that inclined her to follow another path.

THE ARIES BOSS

Very Vocal Υ *Works Fast* Υ *Doesn't Want to Baby-Sit*

Aries won't tolerate your falling asleep with your sunglasses on at your desk. Aries is a prankster, but he will see no humor in your not being man or woman enough to stay alert at work. Anything apathetic in your performance or appearance on the job leaves him testy. Think of the outlaw Butch Cassidy. Do you think for one moment he would have put up with a lackluster Sundance Kid?

Aries wants to see you busy and enterprising. Don't come to him whining that you don't know what to do next. Since he will go out of his way to find a challenge, he likes to think you also can handle your own. He often has high rates of failure along with success. When the Aries fails at something, it is frequently due to his impatience. This is where you can come in and finish the project or assignment for him.

When Aries faces opposition in his work, he becomes Captain Courageous or the warrior and fights failure rather than accepting it. Once again, you can intercede and offer a remedy for the big hairy mess.

Aries appreciates a fast pace, so keep your stupendous work feats coming. One boss I know of chastised an employee for working late on a frequent basis. He equated working late with being slow and unable to keep up. When the worker realized this, he quit taking calls and making presentations after three o'clock, leaving himself two hours to wrap up his day. He was producing less but looking better. It worked for the Aries supervisor. Soon the worker, no longer considered "slow," was rewarded with clients from management.

The Aries boss is not usually good at reading character. Instead, he sees what he wants to see in others. Keep this in mind when he reviews your work. Since the Aries boss always speaks up and speaks out, you won't have to guess about how he feels or what he thinks. Angry, he goes vocal. Still, all in all, Aries is usually a good boss. He often remains friends with his associates long after the project or job is completed.

THE ARIES SEARCH FOR THE "UN"

Philosophy is emerging as one approach to business relationships today. Tom Morris, Ph.D., talks about the new soul of business and the four virtues: truth, goodness, beauty, and unity.

Aries explores the truth. He does this by reaching out for the Un: the unfamiliar, the untried, the unknown. This is where the Aries passion is found, and what motivates and inspires him. His desires and compulsions are to break sound barriers and the rules, go to the extremes, and explore the Uns of the Universe.

ARIES SUCCESS STORIES

Aries' leadership started, I feel sure, with the early cave dwellers and then went on to Romulus, the founder of Rome. Beyond all the early, beginning success stories, there are some more recent ones:

Wilbur Wright, as I mentioned earlier, invented and flew the first airplane. Now, that was confidence.

Gloria Steinem set the record straight on women needing to get control of their own lives and noted, "Some of us are becoming the men we wanted to marry." Her ability to lead started an entire movement for a generation of women. In full Aries tradition, she named her organization NOW. *Now* is an action word. Who would expect less of the Mars-born?

Hugh Hefner showcased his revolutionary personality and started a whole generation of liberated sexual perceptions. While Hefner was certainly at the other end of the spectrum from Ms. Steinem, it is interesting that they both expressed their vocal inclinations in the form of creating a new magazine.

Hefner has been quoted as saying that "*Playboy* was a voice in the wilderness" of publishing. It is that vocal, first-to-speak characteristic again. He also said that his ideas often come to him in the middle of the night. It was in what he called one of his "eureka moments" that he created his Playboy symbol. This is a good example of Aries' random thought process.

Hefner's random way of organizing thoughts is so typical of the Aries. It is also interesting to note that the best ideas do not come nine to five, in an office, or at someone's command for this random thinker. Flextime was invented for the Aries.

Aries is the infant of the zodiac, and it is no surprise that he often accomplishes much early on. Hefner published a penny newspaper at the age of eight. His enterprising and inventive streak displayed itself early on as well. "I was the child who invented the games other people played," he remarked.

In 1998 both Hefner and Steinem were inducted into the Hall of Fame by the Society of Magazine Editors. In a sense, they are the male and female equivalent of each other. Although I am sure the mention of this would start an Aries fire spewing outbursts from either of them.

Elton John has been pounding his chubby fingers on the piano for decades. His incredible talent and his vital, physical approach to music are demonstrated in the way he plays the piano as a true percussion instrument. This in part has made him a true pioneer in the industry.

Johann Sebastian Bach noted that in playing the piano, "There's nothing remarkable about it. All one has to do is hit the right keys at the right time and the instrument plays itself." Who else but someone with physical intelligence would see hitting the keys as the trigger to great compositions?

Ashley Judd is another Aries success story. Ashley displayed the supreme Aries confidence. Undaunted by the country music success of her mother and sister, she did not let comparisons stand in the way of her quest for stardom. Other signs would have quaked at the competition.

Was Rosie O'Donnell afraid of failure entering the world of comedy with no connections and no startling physical beauty? Of course not. Aries is oblivious to limitations.

Pete Rose displayed the remarkable physical intelligence of the Aries. His baseball style was so physically extreme he was nicknamed Charlie Hustle. Known for his fierce temper from time to time, he was, well, vocal. Certainly, he spoke up and out. His love of the game as well as the need for the adrenaline rush in his off-time pursuits demonstrates the sometimes reckless Aries personality on and off the field.

ϒ

OTHER FAMOUS ARIES

Patricia Arquette	David Letterman
Alec Baldwin	Conan O'Brien
Ellen Barkin	Gregory Peck
Jackie Chan	Colin Powell
Francis Ford Coppola	Dennis Quaid
Betty Ford	Richie Sambora
Vince Gill	

RESOURCES

Armstrong, Thomas. 1993. *7 Kinds of Smart*. New York: Penguin Books.

Gardner, Howard. 1993. *Frames of Mind: The Theory of Multiple Intelligences*. New York: Basic Books.

Goleman, Daniel. 1995. *Emotional Intelligence: Why It Can Matter More Than IQ for Character, Health, and Lifelong Achievement*. New York: Bantam Books.

Gregorc, Anthony F. 1982. *An Adult's Guide to Style*. Columbia, CT: Gregorc Associates.

Tobias, Cynthia Ulrich. 1995. *The Way We Work*. Nashville, TN: Broadman and Holman Publishers.

Zehme, Bill. 2000. "A Candid Conversation with the Man," *Playboy Magazine* (January).

CHAPTER 2

THE FINANCIER

TAURUS ■ APRIL 20 TO MAY 21

HOW TO SPOT A TAURUS

Deliberate ♉ *Surefooted*

Taurus meanders through life, rambling slowly around the world of business and profits. Just when you think the race is to the swift, the bull shows up as the symbol of a certain brokerage firm.

The bull is determined and deliberate but not lacking in spontaneity. Plodding and hesitant, he is not usually the first to introduce action. He is surefooted and rather quiet upon first meeting. He is usually dressed tastefully with fine fabrics. You might notice his silk shirts or Bally shoes.

Because the Taurus-born paces himself well, his strength should never be underestimated. It is important to remember that.

Taurus loves luxury and appreciates art and beauty. Conventional, practical, and stable, he is one of the astrological sun signs that can make harmony out of crisis. He wants material gain and is willing to work for it. He often accumulates great wealth as a result. Taurus is not usually forceful in his business presentations or ideas but gracious and soft-spoken.

Known for his loyal and steadfast friendships, Taurus is popular. His approach to work and life is cautious, and his actions are seldom determined by impulse but rather by reflection.

Slow to react or to decide the course of his fate (or yours), Taurus is equally slow to anger. As a rule, anger does not come easily to him, but when enraged he kicks in his heels, makes snorting sounds, and lets his intentions be known. At this point, Taurus usually folds his arms and stands rooted like an old oak tree. When making this stand literally and figuratively, Taurus becomes immovable.

Representing the sign of money, Taurus has been acquiring material possessions since the first beans were counted. He produced crops, made arrangements for rotation, and converted barter from one form of currency to another since the beginning of time.

The extraordinary business savvy of Taurus makes him a natural choice in many ventures. He excels in industries such as insurance, health care management, estate planning, the arts, and music.

WHAT DRIVES THE TAURUS?

The Love of Security ზ *Harmony and Harmonics*

The need for food and shelter propels the Taurus out of his Egyptian cotton monogrammed security blanket and fluffy pillows. The monogramming results from a need to sign his name once again in all transactions. The love of lavishness and toys keeps Taurus motivated by the acquisition of Harleys, Jags, and designer briefcases.

One of the sun signs who is most attracted to creature comforts and material gain, the Taurus finds solace in the things that provide luxury or indulgence. This is why the smell of bread and the texture of chocolate chip cookies are important stimuli to him. Other signs do not even notice these sensations.

To put it simply, Taurus accumulates money to satisfy his five senses.

Years ago, before on-line banking, Richard Mellon was gathering up all the cash, setting up financial institutions, and funding grants. When you think of Taurus, think of William Randolph Hearst, the newspaper and magazine baron, and his immense wealth. Like many other Tauruses, Hearst was, it appeared, destined to make money. Makes you wonder about who built Fort Knox, doesn't it?

The steady, down-to-earth approach of Virgo and Capricorn feels in sync to the Taurus. The deliberate, moseying approach to decisions of his fellow earth signs helps Taurus stay focused and forge ahead with his long-term plans. Taurus, although aware of the moment, always puts tomorrow ahead of today. Taurus has a financial destiny to pursue. Earth signs understand this.

The breezy, superficial approach to business that is often noticeable in the air signs seems to work at cross-purposes for the Taurus. Work styles of the Gemini, Libra, and Aquarius confuse Taurus.

The intuitive Pisces is fascinating to the Taurus who loves the unknown. The water sign's reliance upon "my gut" seems magical to the Taurus who comes only from a fact-driven place. This oddly attracts the Taurus who likes to take an occasional flight of fancy.

The enthusiasm of the fire sign seems to propel Taurus to greater heights. Aries, Leo, and Sagittarius motivate Taurus, when many times he just wants to coast a little, take a break, and read the *Wall Street Journal*.

THE TAURUS WORK STYLE

Comfy ŏ *Ordered* ŏ *Has Time Frames*

Taurus does not work well with a flurry of assignments. He wants a well-structured set of expectations and time frames in which to accomplish tasks. Taurus won't be pushed into something he feels he is not prepared for. He will not be hurried into anything, even a sudden promotion, unless he feels ready to take it on. If you want to make Taurus a partner, suggest a junior partnership first. Give him time to mull it over.

This individual needs a system, an order, and a method to his work. He wants to feel there is value in his job and that he brings integrity to the equation. Taurus does not want to fail in meeting your expectations, or his.

He responds well to praise and takes great pride in his accomplishments. Pragmatic, the Taurus judges success by what he can own and accomplish. The wise coworker or supervisor will take notice of the plaques Taurus has acquired, for his desire to win approval makes praise a natural incentive for him.

THE TAURUS STRENGTHS

Gentle Nature ŏ *Integrity*

Taurus is Taurus. What you see is what you get. He is a stand-up individual, trying not to lose his footing along the corporate way. He has integrity and wants to know that you do also.

Discovering that people he works with do not possess the qualities he's projected on them is shocking and disturbing to the Taurus. The gentle side of his nature hates to be reminded of anything tawdry, arrogant, backbiting, or under the table.

THE TAURUS FAVORITE
WORK ENVIRONMENT

Is Well Appointed ♉ *Incorporates the Earth and Water Elements*

The love of outdoors for walks and fresh air is strong in the Taurus nature, yet he is also happy indoors with executive offices. He likes to be seated behind heavy, ornately carved wood and near signs such as Your Million Dollar Realtor, or Stockbroker of the Year.

No one loves a comfortable office environment more than Taurus. He needs some art, a few cushioned chairs, photos in silver or copper frames. He prefers greens and deep rich European colors. Leather-trimmed appointments and fine writing instruments accessorize his desk. Soft music playing in the background feeds his soul, and he works best when contented and peaceful.

Taurus wants to feel secure in his office. It's all part of his need for a substantial roof over his head. Here is a sun sign that takes feng shui seriously. He prefers his back to the wall and to be facing you. He needs to hear the sound of water and see the foliage of plants near his desk. Taurus is simply trying to bring the beauty and wonder of nature indoors.

Sensitive to hues, he believes that you can change your life with color and lighting. If you question him on this, he will call his lighting color science, which it actually is. He never wants to appear frivolous, only fact-based.

Perhaps Taurus's sensitivity to his surroundings is something the rest of us should strive to be aware of after all.

All this color and sound harmony, even the feng shui, may sound superstitious to you, but the Taurus is acutely aware of sights, sounds, and senses. Never underestimate that. He wants serenity and beauty in his nine-to-five workday and acknowledges all his senses in acquiring tranquility.

27

THE TAURUS EMPLOYEE/COWORKER

Fun ♉ *A Creature of Habit* ♉ *Easygoing* ♉ *Persuasive*

Delightfully funny, Taurus has a strong sense of humor. His laugh can soothe tensions and dissipate anger. Charming, he is almost never confrontational and often allows others too much latitude in overstating a case to him.

His weekends are spent listening to concerts, singing in chorales, exploring the hillsides, or going to the theater. Taurus has black-tie attire in his closet for a reason; most of his weekends are opulent.

A creature of habit, Taurus often repeats favorite vacation time by going back to the familiar rather than making the leap to more exotic excursions. He would rather spend the day in a spa than in Switzerland, unless, of course, he is visiting his Swiss deposits there.

When facing a morale problem, Taurus will take a leisurely lunch and order the richest, fluffiest, whipped cream dessert on the menu. When troubled, Taurus often takes comfort in food.

Upon his return to the office, he will dive into the problem with his sincere little heart. With complete honesty and naïveté, he will tell his superiors and coworkers what is on his mind. Management is not always happy to hear this. Still, his calm presentation, mixed with some self-deprecating humor, rarely creates animosity. The strength of Taurus's negotiation is the complete lack of pretense. He states his terms in just a few clear, concise sentences.

The simplicity in which Taurus wants to live his life, the clarity of his objectives, is almost of another decade. While not the first to be noticed by management, or the quickest with a task, his assent will happen. Taurus is not the meteoric star of the office, but he is the company asset.

Forced by management to do something he finds disagreeable, Taurus will have to be prodded and pushed. Then and only then, he will do it. But, as the old story goes, "the first time shame on you, the second time shame on me." Taurus will be looking in the classifieds or logging onto jobs.com.

A principled individual for the most part, Taurus is a coworker you can trust.

Angered, Taurus is the snorting bull. His feet-stomping refusals are meant to warn you that you just waved the red flag and better back off.

Taurus is a powerful sun sign. He most often displays his power by the art of persuasion. Persuasion is, of course, the ability to get people to do something you want them to do. When Taurus uses his power this way, everyone thinks that they are doing it because they wanted to, not because he suggested it.

Beyond the power of persuasion, Taurus has performance power. Performance power is the ability to accomplish by deciding to do the right things and then doing them at the right time.

THE TAURUS LEARNING STYLE

Is Concrete/Sequential ♉ *Prefers Graphs and Pointers*
Responds to Reinforced Instructions

Everyone and every sign observe the same sights and sounds, yet each perceives these stimuli in different ways. The Taurus learns best when utilizing a style that is concrete.

Taurus uses his heightened sense of sight, smell, touch, taste, and hearing to make judgments. He looks for the tangible and the obvious. With Taurus, what you see is what you get. He sees things as they are; what is, is. He is a black-and-white sort of person, which makes it hard on the greens and grays among us.

The way in which Taurus orders or organizes his perceptions is considered to also represent a sequential learning style. This combination produces a hardworking individual who works by the rules. Taurus by nature is conventional, stable, and dependable. He organizes materials and data in much the same way as he lives his life. He is accurate, factual, and organized. Because of this, he often asks questions to reassure himself he is on the right track.

When comparing him to the traits seen on the Myers-Briggs Vocational Studies Topology, the Taurus is considered to be an introvert and a judge.

Introverts prefer privacy, quiet, and to think things over before they speak. Taurus is quite happy by himself and may even retreat into his office (cave) to recharge his energies.

The judging type of worker likes lists and, to a large degree, routine. Taurus doesn't want a lot of surprises. He has an order for things; he wants pens, pencils, and even those pesky little paper clips in the right place.

Taurus probably has systems for filing, deadlines, and projects that only he can understand. He wants to go through assignments from start to finish. He doesn't mind doing things twice. Each time the Taurus sees something in progress, it reinforces his performance. However, this is not to say he needs or wants repetitive tasks.

If you want to get the attention of a Taurus, send clear and concise memos. When giving a presentation, use a pointer to demonstrate a graph. Instruct him on each point. Organize your presentation for the Taurus, or you risk losing his attention all together.

When Taurus has to repeat a task too often, he will get frustrated. For example, the musical Taurus who is a choral director will become anxious over a long period of time if he needs to change backdrops or sets every week. Even a rock star Taurus will hate the part of the tour where everyone comes in and tears down backdrops and equipment.

Taurus knows the show must go on but in his heart of hearts this part of a musical career is against his nature. Even the likes of Stevie Wonder, Bono, and George Strait most likely feel a certain tension at the end of each performance.

THE TAURUS INTELLIGENCE

The Twin Love of Money and Music ♉ *Musical Intelligence*

Taurus has many talents and forms of intelligence. His primary intelligence is often musical. Taurus's preoccupation with money and tallying up is not in contrast to his musical inclinations.

It is universally agreed that numbers have harmony, and vibrations and music are also mathematical expressions to some degree. Taurus expresses both the mathematical and musical relationships in his work with numbers, counting, and harmony.

Taurus has a way with notes, both musical and banking. He hears music when trying to develop the money card. His emotions are stirred by loose change in his pockets. He is not miserly but generous and, in fact, most often lives lavishly.

Although Taurus is often gifted musically (usually his melodious voice), not all Tauruses can make money in this profession. Still the rhythms and melodies seem to soothe him. This is why background music helps him to concentrate and analyze while working.

Many individuals with musical intelligence find that pursuing music as an avocation or hobby helps them feel fulfilled and in balance.

Philosopher Bertrand Russell suggested that "Mathematics possesses not only truth but supreme beauty." Taurus will tell you he lives for beauty and appreciates it in every form. The correlation is there again regarding Taurus and his two loves.

THE TAURUS PROFILE

Is Sense Oriented ŏ *Likes Checks and Balances*
Likes Strong Leadership

When preparing training sessions for the Taurus, plan presentations with few distractions in comfort-filled, earth-toned rooms with gourmet coffees and croissants. Touch products, hold merchandise in the air, and give out a statuette or the promise of one to capture his attention. Make sure the lighting is subdued.

If you want to work with or for a Taurus, remember he is also of the earth sign elements and of the fixed mode astrologically. This means he is inclined to be stubborn. Fixed signs can be rigid and inflexible once they get an idea in their heads. The best use of the fixed energies, or the positive side of the Taurus nature, is his ability to concentrate—along with his stability of purpose.

The Taurus profile includes his need to gather up things, accumulate, and count. While he works hard toward his goals, a fair degree of material wealth seems to naturally flow to him. Taurus is rarely the lowest-paid employee in the organizational structure.

Preferring to follow, Taurus still manages to become one of the Very Important Persons in any corporation. Taurus frequently ends up being equal to or of parallel significance to the CEO or president. Many ambassadors and several secretaries of state, including Madeline Albright, have been Taurus-born.

Today, many organizations are becoming less structured with fewer tiers of authority. There is widespread scaling down with more mini or independent units. While some sun signs may like the increased freedom, this frightens Taurus.

In addition, the information age is causing us to move faster, which is not something Taurus envisions in his work environment. A fast-paced, independent environment is quite a contrast for the worker who finds a certain comfort in patterns. However, once he considers these changes in commercial and financial terms, Taurus will adapt. He needs to be reassured that faster transactions and lowered overhead costs will increase the bottom line. Remind Taurus of the numbers, and his thinking will undergo a remarkable transformation.

And, it is true, the information age is changing the world of work. The hard data suggest that "going if not yet gone are the nine-to-five workdays; lifetime jobs; predictable, hierarchical relationships; corporate culture security blankets; and for a large and growing sector of the workforce, the workplace itself."

Because of the changing workforce, Taurus will have to rethink his whole security blanket issue. But, he is not inflexible; once he gets the message, he will embrace the change.

The sign of Taurus is the first of the earth signs and is particularly attracted to nature, beauty, and the enjoyment of life. While not a type-B personality, he is predominately introverted and wants to find a balance in his work and life. Taurus wants to enjoy the journey, not just soar through it. He will take the time to smell the roses (oregano, rosemary, and thyme) in life.

Because Taurus appreciates the best, he wants to be the best. When he looks at the Pyramids, Stonehenge, the Great Wall, or his personal favorite, Ft. Knox, Taurus sees something more than beauty and mystery. He notices that these structures were built to last, built to last like the Taurus himself.

Taurus develops long-range strategies. He likes to keep five-year plans handy. He has methods, a system of checks and balances. Taurus wants to hear and see the details of every plan. Taurus is not afraid to ask questions, and he wants answers as well.

THE TAURUS BOSS

Peacemaking ☿ *Reflective* ☿ *Serious About Reprimands*

The ability to create a supportive work environment makes the Taurus a natural supervisor. While he may have food stains on his silk designer shirts, he will not hesitate to correct you on the importance of a misplaced coffee cup on your desk. He likes meticulous surroundings.

Good natured and slow paced, Taurus wants you to be thorough, follow instructions, and get the job done right the first time. He wants to see you as a craftsman at your job and not an assembly sort of person.

Hitting the right musical note, getting the digits to balance, and putting new numbers into the equation, Taurus needs to be precise. He never forgets the necessity to be careful with his assignments.

No one hates to let an employee go more than does a Taurus, which provides a little built-in anti-fire factor. However, his warnings should be taken seriously. Don't think because he is soft-spoken with a hands-off approach that he is a pushover. Just because he does not have his thumb in your back does not mean that he will let anything slide.

A Taurus manager of a large insurance company had an employee who he considered to be passive-aggressive in his billing efforts. Taurus had repeatedly asked for a 6.5-billable-hours report for each day, and this one employee always turned in a 6.2 or 6.3.

The Taurus boss will not let this pass. It is unwise to ignore the warnings of a Taurus supervisor, no matter how nice the reprimand sounds. Listen to his instructions, and don't test his patience. He has calculated that $.2 \times 5 \times 52$ is a whole lot of money, and it's costing a bundle to keep you on board. At this point, it won't be about you; it will be all about numbers.

A certain amount of respect for the dollar comes with this sun sign. Taurus does not squander resources; he simply hates waste. This same boss probably donated a nearly equal amount to a needy family. There is nothing miserly in Taurus's money management. He simply respects the value of it.

When Taurus faces opposition at work, he gets quiet and reflective. Taurus won't charge around yelling, but he will consider how to make changes to accommodate everyone's best interests. Critics may view this as the Taurus way of trying to appease management. Worse, some see him as a "yes" person. He is not. Taurus is simply contemplating the best for all sides.

Despite his calm, placating manner, during upsetting crises, he is seething. Check for yourself, and you will see his nostrils flare in times of upheaval.

Believing success is the best revenge, Taurus finds a way to turn the situation around to his best advantage. Therefore, he rises above the temptation to become petty or bitter.

Here is an individual who is in command and does well in a working relationship where he does not always have to lead the way. When Taurus is in command, he usually surrounds himself with capable associates.

Whenever Taurus makes mistakes in business, it is usually related to someone he has placed in a position of authority. Taurus often selects associates he believes in with a simple faith. Sometimes this blind spot gets Taurus into trouble as his coworkers may not be all he perceives them to be.

TAURUS SUCCESS STORIES

Catherine the Great, who knew all about expanding territory and gaining eventual control, displayed the long-term planning knack of the Taurus.

Ulysses S. Grant, president and the Union Army's great general, exemplifies several Taurus management traits. Grant excelled at math, yet graduated toward the bottom of his class. As a general, he showed the finally enraged Taurus temperament when he negotiated Lee's surrender: "No terms except an unconditional and immediate surrender."

Grant worked well with Lincoln doing what Taurus does best—supporting the main player by being second in command or having parallel power. Some of Grant's greatest problems as president were the associates he surrounded himself with. He continued to believe in his friends and appointees when all evidence pointed to the contrary. This error in judgment caused him much personal and professional grief.

Grant's preoccupation with money is part of his Taurean legacy. Many of Grant's presidential issues were about greenbacks, soft money, hard money, and bank notes. In 1869 he signed the Public Credit Act.

Queen Elizabeth II, one of the richest women in the world, is formidable and astute about power and money. Yet, Elizabeth was born to incredible wealth, as is often the case with Taurus. Recently, she increased her wealth with Internet ventures. Making money still holds that old magic for The Queen.

Barbra Streisand is another Taurus who has the ability and the destiny for enormous wealth. Streisand epitomizes the musical intelligence of the Taurus, as do Cher and other musically talented Taureans such as Duke Ellington, Zubin Mehta, and many operatic performers.

Comedian Jerry Seinfeld's preoccupation with numbers was at the root of his retirement from his series. He reflected on the importance of the number nine and its relationship to the end of a cycle in numerology. For Seinfeld, nine meant time to quit.

There is a certain magic of numbers that we all should recognize. In physics the magic numbers are: 2, 6, 8, 14, 20, 28, 50, 82, and 126. Pass this on to your Taurus coworker, and let him figure out the whole thing. Perhaps he will weave them into his financial destiny.

Bono, of U2, illustrates the Taurean love of the musical, mathematical, and monetary by his founding Jubilee 2000, an organization for Third World debt relief. His work involves visits to presidents, world leaders, Wall Street, and the favorite Taurean haunt, the Treasury Department. Part of his passion may be inspired by the intrigue of the sheer numbers of the debt, millions and billions.

Barbra Streisand's Foundations have been giving grants since 1986 for environmental problems. Her grants are in the high six figures, and some year's grants total one million dollars. Many other Tauruses are found campaigning for global issues and concerns.

Taurus at his gold-dusted, big-hearted best is the grantor, donor, and benefactor.

☿

OTHER FAMOUS TAURUSES

Valerie Bertinelli	Shirley MacLaine
Pierce Brosnan	Jack Nicholson
Joe Cocker	Al Pacino
Tony Danza	Gabriela Sabatini
Nora Ephron	Aaron Spelling
Janet Jackson	Tori Spelling
Andie MacDowell	

RESOURCES

The American Heritage Dictionary, 2nd College Edition. 1985. Boston, MA: Houghton Mifflin.

Funkhouser, G. Ray. 1986. *The Power of Persuasion: A Guide to Moving Ahead in Business and Life*. New York: Houghton Mifflin.

Gregorc, Anthony F. 1982. *An Adult's Guide to Style*. Columbia, CT: Gregorc Associates.

Kroeger, Otto, and Janet M. Thuesen. 1988. *Type Talk*. New York: Tilden Press.

Miner, Margaret, and Hugh Rawson. 1994. *The New International Dictionary of Quotations*. New York: Signet Books.

O'Hara-Deveraux, Mary, and Robert Johansen. 1994. *Global/Work: Bridging Distance, Culture and Time*. Dallas, TX: Jossey-Bass Management.

CHAPTER 3

THE COMMUNICATOR

GEMINI ▪ MAY 21 TO JUNE 22

HOW TO SPOT A GEMINI

Quick-Witted Ⅱ *Chameleon*

Gemini dashes around, light-footed and darting. He often seems to be going in opposite directions or circles to get to his many destinations. Right after the handshake and introduction, Gemini talks of "I and me," or "we thought." Gemini is never one, but two personalities.

Gemini's most notable traits are his restless, talkative, and quick-witted nature. He is often multidimensional, bilingual, and bicoastal. Whoever said, "You can pretend to be serious, but you can't pretend to be witty," hadn't met Gemini, because Gemini can be both. Or pretend to be both. One is never sure with Gemini.

Every individual is unique, and like snowflakes, no two of us are alike. We are all capable of showing different sides and views of ourselves throughout our lives. Only Gemini can do this daily: radio announcer by day, concert pianist by night, introvert by day, extrovert by night. Gemini is the chameleon of the zodiac. He is likeable and popular in every hour, however.

Gemini is often ambidextrous, hyperactive, and chatty. He is a master of conversation. A Gemini's life is an adventure, a travelogue, and his quest is to enjoy the journey. Gemini can lead or follow, but he mingles best. It is important to remember that when working with one.

Some of Gemini's most notable characteristics are his ever-changing expressions, interests, and, yes, residences or vocations. The Gemini's natural-born ability to adapt provides him with the perfect character to move up or down the corporate ladder. He is never one to get stuck on a rung.

Gemini has been communicating since the beginning of time: sending out smoke signals, inscribing on walls and coconut shells, wandering in tribes, and in more recent times, organizing groups in offices all over the world.

Gemini's decisions are not ruled by impulse or reflection but by quantum leaps of logic, his mind-boggling reasoning a predicament for the Gemini of yesteryears. But in the E-days of 2000 and beyond, it will be one of his most sought-after business qualities.

Is it Donald Trump's billions or his image of billions that enables him to live like one of the richest men in the world? Was it his nothing-down real estate deals that made him a model for land and real estate ventures? Or did he put down a million dollars on Mar-a-Lago after all? Even the Gemini is not certain of his actual circumstances on occasion.

For you see, while some signs actually reinvent themselves, Gemini re-creates himself. There is a difference. Gemini rewrites his history from time to time when necessary to take a huge social leap or an enormous career move.

In the world of business speak, Gemini is the megaphone. When Gemini makes mistakes in commerce, it usually relates to something misspoken, misquoted, misdirected. A misstep in his personal quantum physics of communications is the most common downfall of the Gemini.

Of course, there is no down in downfall for Gemini. He is "Mr. Up and Down" or as Gemini Vince Lombardi was nicknamed, "Mr.

Hi and Low." Geminis are mercurial in moods, career paths, and destinations.

Once Gemini has made up his mind(s), he is quick to implement his decisions. He may hate to put his determinations in writing, let alone carve them in stone. He knows full well his path is not linear, nor is his planning.

This nonlinear thinking so typical of Gemini can be a good thing for everyone in an organization. It is just this sort of unlimited, expansive ability to live out an idea in his head that produced the likes of Frank Lloyd Wright.

Imagine the originality of all glass doors and metal furniture in 1904 as Wright did. Rather a transposition in the beginning of modern architecture, wasn't it? Gemini is always fooling with form and geometry of thought.

While it is the mind that captures the prizes for the Gemini (many Nobel winners are Gemini), it is also the body that wins Wimbledon, sprinting and swimming championships, golf tournaments. Like everything else about Gemini, his talents come in pairs.

Gemini is most often the mind and body of the zodiac. The heart and soul is dominated by other sun signs. If you are looking for in-depth, esoteric musings, look elsewhere.

Gemini excels in integrating ideas and motion. As a result, he is often a writer, teacher, lecturer, radio announcer, songwriter, as well as one of the natural-born athletes of any generation.

WHAT DRIVES THE GEMINI?

The Search for Knowledge ♊ *Mental Stimulus* ♊ *The Need to Verbalize*

The need for expression and movement gets the Gemini to produce something other than profits for planet "mundanity," or planet Earth to the rest of us. Gemini is not motivated by material gain, but by the pursuit of it. It is the thrill of the chase that propels him out of the lows and into the high-soaring flights of fancy.

Since his imagination knows no limits, his boundaries are infinity. Whatever he achieves is often not quite enough. After all, he is doing this for the two of him.

The earthy Taurus, Virgo, and Capricorn often make a nice companionable match, but Gemini finds them constricting. The need of earth signs for definition, boundaries, and structure makes Gemini feel hampered, all cramped up in the mind. Still, earth signs can take the notes and put them into form and categories, or at least put a name to the concept.

Ideas, forms, and knowledge are the primary motivators of Gemini. He is often scattered in his search for growth and information, and can appear to be superficial as a result. Still, the quest for knowledge is what inclines the Gemini to his excellent potential.

Around 400 or 500 B.C., two Geminis were also talking, chatting up the neighborhoods: Socrates and Plato are considered two of the great thinkers in Western civilization. Gemini always talks, writes, lectures, and teaches.

Gemini is usually proficient in two or more vocations or talents. For example, Socrates was educated in literature but was also a gymnast. He was popular and had a great sense of humor. Socrates talked to just about anybody who listened. He did not like to put his work into written form, however. This is something to remember about Gemini when you are looking for someone to help on the annual report.

Plato is perhaps more exceptional than the Gemini you just met at the chamber mixer. Then again, he may not be. But, Plato demonstrated what passions drive the complex Gemini.

In Plato's *Nature of Forms*, he theorized about form: circularity, squareness, and triangularity. Plato went on to pursue social ethics and eventfully wrote some things down. Most of his writing was in the form of dialogues and letters, however, the preferred communication style of Gemini.

Plato defined virtues when compared to class structure via four states: temperance, courage, wisdom, and justice. All his theories, his pondering, his forehead-rubbing ideas related to the educational process and man's search for knowledge.

So while you may not work with one of the great thinkers when you work with Gemini, you do work with a prototype or work in progress. It is wise to remember that Gemini is an analytical creature and his ideas are constantly changing. You will hear a lot about possibilities whenever you are around Gemini.

Gemini is an out-of-the-box thinker, way out of the box. While his ideas may sound like endless prattle to some, it is the food that feeds his soul. Like alphabet soup for kids.

The fire signs Aries, Leo, and Sagittarius can act out the ideas and orate and publish the speeches for Gemini. Gemini can get along splendidly with Aries and Leo, in spite of all the fuss and opposition between the two of them. The Sagittarian can take any Gemini concept global. Sagittarius won't let Gemini leave his great ideas to lie in a heap. Sagittarius will pack them up, put them on the road, take them to laboratories, or put them on the Internet.

Fellow air signs such as Gemini understand the life of an idea before it is ever spoken, written, or captured in any concrete way. Libra and Aquarius help the Gemini find application of his work and expand it for humanity. The air signs will understand the search for virtues, which is an underlying fire.

Air and water can give us clouds, bubbles, and things that burst. Gemini senses this and is often reluctant to let the water signs dampen his spirit.

THE GEMINI STRENGTHS

A Natural for E-Commerce ♊ *Attracts Solutions*

Gemini brings his own special brand of enlightenment to this generation. He is entertaining, convincing, verbal, and is a natural for the E-commerce environment.

Gemini can attract solutions and answers. He has potential that is ripe for the Information Age. He is resourceful and can make leaps of logic as solid as a bridge. Gemini is not afraid to go to the edge of his capabilities.

THE GEMINI FAVORITE WORK ENVIRONMENT

Is Individualized ♊ *Incorporates Other Facets of His Life*

Gemini loves color and objects with shape and form. His office is often modern or retro but always picturesque.

Vince Lombardi, one of the "winningest" coaches in football history, used his office to make a statement. He chose a masculine tone, formal, a little foreboding. He used tan burlap wallpaper to send a message that this was a man's domain. One of his accessories was a dartboard on the wall, no doubt used to vent his frustration while waiting between appointments.

A Gemini woman I know whose hobby is reading decorated her office with a room divider of hand-painted books and placed a chair from her late father's den in the corner. On the desktop there were a few rolls of film and off in the corner a yellow candle and some honeysuckle.

Family mementos and reminders of avocations are usually part of the Gemini's decor. President John Kennedy had his famous rocking chair. It was said he used it as a way to dissipate some of his nervous energy. Perhaps it reminded him of a childhood memory.

THE GEMINI EMPLOYEE/COWORKER

Persuasive ♊ *Changeable* ♊ *Analytical*

Gemini is popular. His inclination to mingle extends to his coworker's lives. He merges divisions, titles, and managerial styles in the most innocuous of ways. He organizes company picnics, knows important dates of his work pals. Remembering Mr. Jones's dog's surgery or Miss Smith's promotional evaluation date is as meaningful to him as it is insignificant to others.

Gemini's weekends are spent cross-country skiing, at swimming matches, and as soccer mom. A few will pursue a part-time vocation or avocation, such as freelance photography.

Prone to adventure seeking, Gemini reads about travel and dreams of climbing in Tibet next May. Gemini would rather be in the midst of any physical challenge than pursue a mild-mannered, elegant vacation.

Gemini, when facing a morale problem, tries to talk it out. Persuasive, he is glib, smooth, and if need be, will verbalize you into submission. Gemini can sell the concepts of not working overtime and increasing productivity at the same time. Is that incongruous? Gemini will have an explanation.

Wherever he is employed, Gemini encourages the buddy system and masterminds a new atmosphere. He is often ingenious. A natural salesperson, Gemini can sell anything. It should not surprise you that he will sell changes in the organization. First thing you know, the deal is done and management is patting itself on the back for Gemini's ideas, never suspecting where the change originated.

Gemini is complicated yet appears superficial. He is witty and energetic with seemingly boundless energy. Actually he is driven by demons of restlessness and often is fatigued. Sometimes, when he is tired and snappish, he shows his other side.

Because Gemini is absorbing information at the speed of light, he is changeable. Like the lines in *I Ching*, Gemini is his own book of changes. He is in a constant state of movement and, therefore, is not easily stilled.

Propelled by change, Gemini is not a predictable worker. Don't count on him being there long enough to collect the gold watch. It will take more than that to interest him in being a company person.

Gemini needs stimulation, potential, opportunity, and recognition for his cleverness to keep him behind any desk or any CEO. He must also be allowed to turn 180 degrees every now and then without enduring name calling, such as traitor or turncoat.

Don't take his every conjecture or theory to heart. He was just thinking out loud after all.

THE GEMINI LEARNING STYLE

Abstract II *Sequential* II *Quick*

Everyone and every sign observe the same sights and sounds, yet each perceives them in different ways. While at some level we all see what we expect to see, we still convert information in two distinct fashions. One perceptual quality is an abstract learning style. This is how the Gemini's mind most often works.

As you know by now, Gemini thinks in the conceptual realm. He likes to work with possibilities and what can be. He loves to look at the angles, the circles, and the forms. Gathering information, indeed creating it, is important to Gemini.

It should not surprise you that Gemini needs to gather twice as much information as other signs. He asks multiple questions. Sometimes his need to ask exceeds his instructor's or supervisor's patience.

The way in which Gemini orders his information is considered to be sequential. While Gemini's thought process might seem random to most of us, he does think in an ordered fashion. It is just not always apparent on the outside. Indeed, Gemini often shows a deliberate side that confuses many other sun signs.

Gemini has the gift of being able to conceptualize ideas. Primarily a person of logic and reason, he effortlessly perceives things in his head before any idea is put to pencil.

Gemini is both an extrovert and an introvert. Happy by himself to research his pet theories, he is also eager to explain everything to anyone who will listen.

When viewed in the context of some vocational testing instruments, Gemini is a thinker. Although he is as verbal as a dictionary and reasons quickly, he may decide slowly. Such is the dichotomy of Gemini. Just when you think he is fast, he is slow.

THE GEMINI INTELLIGENCE

Usually Rewarded in Business Ⅱ *Highly Verbal*

Gemini has many talents and forms of intelligence. His primary intelligence is often linguistic, and thus verbal. Writers, teachers, poets (such as Ralph Waldo Emerson) are often Gemini-born.

Gemini usually has a large vocabulary and is good at word games. Because of this, he excels in debates or opening statements. Good at trivia, he evolves into the scholar and can be one of the most innovative thinkers.

Society has rewarded and recognized the linguistic, verbal intelligence since the earliest of times. Because of this, Gemini is often credited with more intelligence than he possesses.

As a culture, we use the linguistic intelligence as a standard and are just now discovering that other forms of intelligence are also valuable, if less measurable. Still, this IQ measurement gives Gemini a chance to make early starts and show early promise.

THE GEMINI PROFILE

Negotiates Freely Ⅱ *Is Fearless*

Gemini likes everything analyzed, accounted for, in order, and labeled, if only in his mind. Being resourceful, he can transform the uninspired, defeated, and sluggish with his talk of actualization.

Vince Lombardi had no tolerance for the unenthusiastic and told his players to talk, look, and act like the winners they would become. His approach to coaching was typical of Gemini.

"You must pound the lessons into the players by rote, the same way you teach pupils in the classroom," Lombardi advised. Gemini, for all his popularity and dizzying superficial chitchat, can be, and often is, relentless in the pursuit of his dreams.

Whether in the classroom, the forum, the senate, or the Oval Office, Gemini uses his mind to lead the way. In his Inaugural Address in 1961, John F. Kennedy reminded us to "never negotiate out of fear, but let us never fear to negotiate." This summarizes the Gemini negotiating style.

As we move from the Industrial Age to the Information Age, Gemini fearlessly crosses new boundaries and relishes in the increased freedom in working environments. And he is fond of remote or distance working.

In decades past, organizations held the power, but the trend now is for individuals to hold the power. Once Gemini grasps this concept, he will be as free to express himself as his ancient pals Socrates, Plato, and the person sending out smoke signals from the top of the hill.

THE GEMINI BOSS

Subject to Mood Swings ♊ *Wants You to Be Accountable*

Gemini is always a favorite in the workforce. Not every day, of course. That would be too much to hope for. You must expect days when he will barely notice you, or then again take exception to you and your work.

Still, Gemini is a likable boss who wants you to accept that his role is to change things, create new policies, and reinvent the wheel. It is wise not to mention that "Ms. Supervisor-before-him" did it the other way, or that it has always been done this way. This is not how Gemini works.

You can expect quick office visits, unexpected E-mails, calls in flight, and new procedure manuals. While Gemini is not necessarily touchy-feely, he is nearby. Just when you think it is safe to log on to your favorite website, he reappears. He has an unusual level of awareness.

Gemini will make you accountable. He will ask you to make presentations and evaluations, and he will expect you to know his staff on a first-name basis as he does. The faster you absorb information, the more responsive he will be to your advancement in his organization.

Gemini does not like to stay too long in any one place or to be required to submit reports and tedious details to his boss. For this reason, the people the Gemini Boss surrounds himself with are associates who excel at the things he fights against, such as restraints and accountability.

THE GEMINI SEARCH FOR ETHICS

The great contradiction of Gemini is that while he most often has a superficial approach to many things, he wants a deeper understanding of life.

While Gemini is not the most soul-searching of the sun signs, he is intrigued by questions of ethics and morality. Plato expressed it well in his conclusion that it is the moral person who is truly the happy person. Gemini wants to be as happy as he appears.

GEMINI SUCCESS STORIES

Kenneth Geddes Wilson, a Nobel Prize winner in physics, was fascinated by how bulk matter undergoes changes. He questioned why water goes from solid to liquid via temperature changes and solved this riddle in his phase transition theory. Gemini always has a theory.

Gemini is always fascinated by change, and when he utilizes his insights in conversion and alterations within a work environment, he makes some of his most important corporate contributions. As a result, Gemini is often a successful business consultant.

President John F. Kennedy embodied many of the Gemini traits. He was very popular, verbal, quick-witted, and intelligent. Kennedy was athletic and primarily swam and sailed. He was an avid reader and successful writer, and one of his books won the Pulitzer Prize.

Like countless other Geminis before and after him, Kennedy's linguistic intelligence proved to be his most valuable asset in business. Kennedy proved his linguistic superiority in his debates with Richard Nixon, and many think this skill helped him win the presidential election. The Gemini dialectic talent has always been strong.

When PT Boat 109 was sliced in two, Kennedy and his crew clung to the wreckage. Later he carved a message on a coconut shell that helped rescuers find him and his crew. Always the communicator, Gemini has carved out primitive messages for centuries. It is second nature to him.

Kennedy surrounded himself with advisers who were some of the great thinkers of his time. Many of his appointees were teachers and scholars. Gemini is always comfortable with talking heads, scholars, and instructors.

A supporter of big business, Kennedy somehow managed to get himself branded "anti-business." So very Gemini, this name-calling turn of events.

The often hidden, poetic nature of Gemini is revealed in Kennedy's comment, "When power corrupts, poetry cleanses." This is Gemini, at his incongruous best.

⚊

OTHER FAMOUS GEMINIS

George H. W. Bush	Greg Kinnear
Naomi Campbell	Paul McCartney
Courteney Cox	Marilyn Monroe
Clint Eastwood	Prince Phillip
John Goodman	Priscilla Presley
Bob Hope	Brooke Shields
Helen Hunt	Will Smith
Wynonna Judd	

RESOURCES

Maraniss, David. 1999. "Lombardi's Way," *Vanity Fair* (September).

Miner, Margaret, and Hugh Rawson. 1994. "The Kennedy speech of October 26, 1963," *The New International Dictionary of Quotations*. New York: Signet Books.

CHAPTER 4

THE COUNSELOR

CANCER ■ JUNE 22 TO JULY 23

HOW TO SPOT A CANCER

Sensitive ♋ *Intuitive*

Cancer is a little uncertain or hesitant in his walk. He pauses, looks around, slides his foot left, then to the right, and pauses again. Cancer is tentative; if only adhesive were on the ground. Every venture seems a little iffy, untried, and of an experimental nature. Cancer approaches life like he walks. Don't let him fool you; he will have a bold finish in the world of business.

Cancer is sensitive, brooding, emotional, and imaginative. Security and home are of utmost importance to him. Like the phases of his ruler the moon, Cancer's moods change regularly.

One of Cancer's most notable characteristics is that while he seems to be uncertain, he is actually one of the initiating, driven signs of the zodiac. Cancer only appears reluctant about expressing the force of his ambitions in the early part of his life.

Cancer, ruled by the moon and the seas, is sensitive to the elements. Nurturing families for centuries, Cancer is the matriarch of the zodiac. Cancer's natural love of genealogy, family, and heritage makes him the one to perpetuate lineage and tradition in society. This personal destiny, related to culture and ancient wisdom, often extends into the world of work.

When Cancer comes to work, he views his work environment as his extended family. He no doubt was one of the originators of the company picnic, day-care facilities, and take-your-daughter-to-workday activities.

If you have not yet worked with Cancer and you do not see how these descriptions apply, think of Princess Diana: her well publicized moods; the perpetuation of bloodlines, which was clearly a part of her fate; and the extended family as she became the people's princess. She exemplified the Cancer across the desk from you. He just has no tiara.

Cancer always has a sense of destiny. If it is not the kismet of ancestry and family, then he will become the entrepreneur who makes provisions for unborn Cancer heirs.

Cancer is the sign of many billionaires. John D. Rockefeller, who set the stage for so many other family lives and fortunes, was a Cancer. The enormity of his wealth guaranteed that future inheritors were entitled to many silver-spoon opportunities. He also secured a place for them in society.

President George W. Bush stepped into the political arena, backed by his *Mayflower* ancestors, assured of a future in politics and a place in history. Lineage is an important ingredient in Cancer's work style. He brings the past and future to work with him every day.

Countless Cancers without titles exist in the world of business, acting out similar life dramas and being loved through it all. Cancer is receptive and has an inborn sense about people. Because of this ability, he is always appreciated and liked.

Titles, lineage, and privilege or not, it does not matter really; the Cancer is often a spectacular success story. He shows an inkling of his potential at an early age, when he sells his toys at a family garage sale.

A tally in *Who's Who* shows an inordinate amount of Cancers listed throughout history. Even before we had Blue Books, Blue Blood, and Blue Stocks, Cancer was the emperor, the king or queen.

Several signatures on the Declaration of Independence belong to our founding fathers, many of whom were Cancers. Most often, heads of nations or founding nations are Cancers.

While Cancer doesn't like to work with numbers, he could instinctively assess my *Who's Who* theory. One of Cancer's talents is that he can add numbers in his head. Cancer has the gift of what I call "Magic Math," which is the ability to guesstimate. Cancer's estimate is usually right on target and guided by intuition. This sort of inner guidance may be what leads Cancer to many wonderful opportunities.

Most of Cancer's success comes in fields of counseling, psychiatry, and writing. Cancers excel as historians, statespersons, labor union leaders, managers and administrators, and even a few famous preachers along the way. They gravitate toward any career that lands them at the helm.

WHAT DRIVES THE CANCER?

Intuition ♋ *His Loved Ones* ♋ *Personal Destiny*

Emotions rule the Cancer. Still, wanting to do the right thing for his loved ones usually requires leadership; as a result, leadership becomes Cancer's secondary motive.

Cancer comes from an instinctual place. His decisions are inner directed. This is not to say that he does not carefully consider input from his coworkers, but Cancer relies on facts with a little pinch of ESP or a whiff of sixth sense. This receptivity is what opened the sightless eyes of Helen Keller to the world of the sighted.

Often Cancer makes his conclusions based on what this will do for the group as a whole. His decisions are rarely all about him. For this reason, he is often a favored supervisor.

The earth signs of Virgo, Capricorn, and especially Taurus work well with Cancer. However, often the mixture of water and earth is, well, muddy. Things will have to gel or settle awhile before the results can be assessed. Not the quick teams as a rule, their finest hours come after a longer period of working together.

The fire signs of Aries, Leo, and Sagittarius are frequently taxing for Cancer. To Cancer, Aries energies appear combative, Leo demanding, and Sagittarius blunt. The sensitive nature of Cancer is often at odds with the blazing energies of the fire signs.

The air signs of Gemini, Libra, and Aquarius appeal to the Cancer intellect. He knows while he is more intuitive, the air signs possess ideas that he can utilize. Cancer loves to convert the concepts of others for his own use. Cancer senses that somehow both he and the air signs understand theories in an unusual manner.

Cancer's fellow water signs, Scorpio and Pisces, are simply wonderful in certain circumstances, such as research, medical professions, and collaborations. Other times, they can be too much of a good thing—too much feeling, emotion, gut-level decisions. Cancer frequently needs reinforcements from some of the more analytical earth signs such as Virgo.

THE CANCER WORK STYLE

Leads ♋ *Manipulates* ♋ *Nurtures* ♋ *Inspires Loyalty*

Cancer wants a working environment that stresses personal attention. He wants praise, understanding, and nurturing. He prefers tasks that encourage him to solve problems or use his people skills. He is manipulative and will have his employer espousing the Cancer theories as his own, forgetting their origin. Like water flowing over gaps and rough edges of any surface, Cancer is smooth.

Since Cancer has been leading us for eons, you should not be surprised that he usually commands at work or that he may become your boss. In fact, you might prepare for it. Some Cancers lead without titles for years. They inspire loyalty that cannot be orchestrated.

Cancer does best when given the chance to help others, to improve morale, and to give credit for jobs well done. He will fight for changes when he believes it is for everyone's best interest.

THE CANCER STRENGTHS

Interpersonal Intelligence ♋ *Empathy*

In a word, feelings. Cancer wants to meet with people, to be a part of history, to measure his lifetime by events such as marriage, children, meeting with people, developing enterprise. He wants his involvement with people and organizations to be positive. He wants to feel good about what he does and who he is.

Cancer has a genuine interest in others, and due to this he is the office glue. Cancer does not fear change; he senses it before official announcements and policy revisions are made.

Since Cancer gets along unusually well with others, he is a near necessity in any organization. He knows instinctively how to mentor, motivate, and lead others. He excels in praising efforts, nurturing apprentices, lending the corporate helping hand, all traits of the successful.

When preparing training sessions for the Cancer, plan presentations in small, intimate groups. Encourage introductions that are personal. Have everyone bring pot lunch, and don't let him get too hungry. Cancer's moods can be dictated by his stomach. Ask Cancer for his feelings on the subject at hand. Let him express himself at his own pace. Remember, he is hesitant only in the early part of his career.

THE CANCER FAVORITE WORK ENVIRONMENT

Acknowledges Chi ♋ *Reminds Him of Home*

Cancer is happy with home-based businesses, which is how the famous Estee Lauder started her business. Although Cancer's business may not stay small, the philosophy often does.

Corporate retreats in familiar settings find Cancer at his productive best. Offices that overlook the ocean, or at least an aquarium or koi pond, suit him, as does soothing music. This may appear overstated for the Cancer. But if you understand Chi, it is the Cancer who catches a glimmer of his destiny long before the rest of us do; he does this in part because he is in touch with the energies of the universe.

Chi is part of the cosmic breath, our energy, and it is part of how Cancer affects his workplace. Cancer has memories of the womb. Don't let the plaque of fishing lures or sand paintings fool you. He carries a solid force to the work arena.

Cancer brings family photos to work. Pictures of grandparents and children are noticeable. He wants continuity in his life. He needs an office that is part home.

THE CANCER EMPLOYEE/COWORKER

Works Best in Small Groups ⊚ *Knows All Your Secrets*
Wants the Gold Watch ⊚ *Does Not Like Extended,*
Out-of-Town Assignments

Cancer is in your organization for the long haul. Leaving his job is rather like facing being adopted into a new family and the adjustment is difficult for him. He bonds where he works. He wants to stay. He wants to keep his job. He has kept all the ribbons from the company races. But, if you don't give him positive reinforcement for his work or financial rewards, you can expect an exodus.

The exodus won't just be the Cancer employee, but his loyal followers. At least one or two, anyway.

Cancer is tenacious and persevering, but not without spunk. He does not want extended out-of-town training sessions or phone limitations that restrict all communication with his family during the day. He must be allowed a little time to touch base with his home or loved ones daily. Turning a blind eye to this quirk of his may be your best strategy.

While the Cancer employee is not excited by changes, he will adapt. He is not afraid to make changes in personnel or corporate structure. Cancer must feel that the change is for the good of the whole organization, that no one is slighted or hurt in the process. He is hypersensitive himself and is anxious to please others.

Cancer lives such a careful blend of home and office that his weekends are often spent with coworkers, working overtime in the office, or checking voice mail. He is never too far removed from his work.

Watching history channels, reading Civil War novels, going to antique shows are ways in which he relaxes. He may sort through old boxes and family mementos or make elaborate plans to redecorate the house. For Cancer the home is the single most important thing in his life.

When Cancer is relaxing, he is one of the funniest people around. While he is hesitant about a number of things, he is quick-witted with his sense of humor. He will make up names for you and your children that are endearing. You become "Mr. Smith and his Elegant Wife," or "Princess Tiger" after you wore the print to work.

Cancer, who will know all your secrets, will tell you few of his. He keeps his heartaches to himself. He does not ask that his coworkers are perfect, just honorable and loyal.

Cancer is a driving force and comfy as old shoes. This is the reason he is hard to partner with; just when you think you're palling around in business, Cancer demands an audit.

Don't get carried away with the impression that Cancer is totally emotion based and harmlessly all warm and fuzzy; he has a calculating side. Like his ruler the moon, Cancer has a dark side. "Everyone is a moon and has a dark side which he never shows to anyone." Never more true than with Cancer.

A couple I know, in business together, are friends and both happily married—just not to each other. It may surprise you that they regularly attend counseling sessions for their business. It may not surprise you that their business is counseling based.

This dynamic duo met working for an international medical firm. They had different work styles but knew they were a talented team. So they left the firm and now head a top-rated medical counseling firm in a large city.

The man, a Virgo, complains that they spend all their time at the counselor's, trying to explain what they need from each other. They gave up on memos long ago. A perfectionist with tremendous business organizational skills, he may be one of the only therapists on the planet who types his case notes until one in the morning.

She on the other hand, a Cancer, forgets to use the client logs and is always behind on her progress reports and monthly evaluations. But, her clients are awed by her ability to understand their needs and help them get what they want from their sessions and for their lives.

Each business partner realizes that without the other this business would not be successful. He lacks the insights to be a Freud, and she lacks the preparation to be remotely ready for a state audit. Yet for all her deficiencies in the paperwork department, the Cancer will turn right around and ask her partner for an accounting. This drives him to howling like a mad dog.

To their credit, the first priority of these partners is to maintain their friendship and respect for each other. And for her, she needs the intimacy, the feel of the family unit in order to produce her magical work and results.

Cancer does best when working in small groups and sharing ideas or brainstorming. This is why Cancer prefers limited partners or a close-knit corporate board.

THE CANCER LEARNING STYLE

Perceptive ⊚ *Driven by Imagination*

The way a Cancer learns, or the way in which his mind works, is considered abstract when viewed in the context of the Gregorc Model of Learning Styles.

Everyone and every sign observe the same sights and sounds, yet each perceives them in different ways. While at some level we all see what we want to see, we still convert information in two distinct fashions. One perceptual quality is abstraction.

When you think or perceive in an abstract way, you need to register the world around you in ways that allow for creative visualization. Cancer can understand ideas and information he cannot actually see or touch. He comes from a place of imagination and feelings. He sees implications, possibilities, and potentials. He registers, from the subtleties in his environment, information that others ignore.

For example, Cancer sees the future from a glance, or a glimmer of information. He reads between the lines and often interprets subtle body language clues from you. Cancer wants to search for a deeper meaning, or the obscure. He does not need the immediate or the instant. He can and will wait for that right opportunity, that chance moment, or destiny's lead.

You can present information to the Cancer without a database, based on an assumption, and generate his excitement with words that tell of likelihood and time frames in the future.

When making presentations in training sessions, try reading, writing, and role-playing to get Cancer's attention. Interaction with others is a sure way to spark his interest in any subject. When making a presentation for a proposal, you can skip steps in procedures and dismiss formalities. Just show the Cancer the end result.

The second component to learning is how we order our information. Cancer prefers unstructured, quick methods of organization, which is called a random learning style. Cancer learns better when allowed to be spontaneous, imaginative, and flexible. Let him brainstorm. Let him fail his way to success with creative experiments and innovations. This is the path of the true entrepreneur.

Cancer does not need physical evidence to brainstorm, and he does best when learning is related to his frame of reference.

Remember, it only appears that Cancer does not have a plan.

THE BEST WAY FOR A CANCER TO LEARN

Brainstorming Is Encouraged ♋ *He Is Given Positive Feedback*

Cancer is highly sensitive and all learning feels part of a personal experience to him. If a subject does not hold any interest for Cancer, or does not appear to have an effect on his life or the lives that matter most to him, he will not be an attentive learner.

Cancer pursues knowledge for the love of it. For this reason, prerequisites are not of particular importance to him. The certifications to satisfy an employer will not really demonstrate his potential. He may even perform poorly, below his abilities, due to lack of interest.

Cancer does not do well when he feels he has no control over the environment. He wants to at least have access to the air conditioning switches, the chance to eliminate tensions between coworkers, and a choice about who to work with. Team him up with inharmonious partners for demonstrations and mock presentations and he gets sullen, remote.

Cancer is one of the most caring and nurturing of the twelve zodiac signs. Therefore, he learns best when subjects are presented in a way that appeals to his need to ultimately further the well-being of others.

Cancer most often excels in the service and helping industries. He likes spontaneity in learning and to feel a connection with instructors and other students or participants.

While Cancer may not be excited by changes, he will adapt. He is not afraid to make changes or be assigned new tasks, just hesitant. Sensitive, he does best with positive reinforcements. Negative comments made to or about him are like missiles to his heart.

Cancer is predominately right-brained and perceptive. While management cannot cater to those functioning best with the right side of the brain exclusively, many top management companies can and do allow for the emotional side of their employees. They often do so by offering support and small celebrations such as personal holidays, casual days, and gift giving.

Cancer does well in small divisions and with intimate teams. Allow a Cancer to express his intuitive and creative ideas, and he creates stellar job performances.

Give the Cancer the chance to present ideas to express his personal thoughts on a project. Often his super success idea is related to another that is behind or ahead of the concept that fell from the top of his head to his mouth. Cooperate with him in the same way that he cooperates with the rest of the staff, and the crab will flourish.

A team player, Cancer needs to feel his extended family at work is anticipating his success. He anticipates it. It is a complex and fast-changing world. Trust that his instincts, his intuitive leaps, will be his greatest company asset.

THE CANCER INTELLIGENCE

Interpersonal ⊙⊙ *Gift of Understanding*

The Cancer intelligence, interpersonal in nature, is related to empathy and the gift of understanding others and what they want and need.

Interpersonal IQ is often associated with individuals who get along unusually well with others. Their extraordinary people skills make them a necessity in any organization. They know instinctively how to mentor, motivate, and lead others. Cancer is adept in praising efforts, nurturing apprentices, and lending the corporate helping hand.

If you want to work with or for a Cancer, remember he is an abstract/random, right-brained, interpersonal personality.

Cancer is also of the water element and cardinal mode astrologically, which means he will always find a way to lead and inspire and to overcome problems.

Cancer is the first of the water signs and is predominately introverted according to vocational measurements by characteristics. A notable characteristic of the introverted, or introspective, Cancer is his need to get off and recharge his soul. He also possesses a certain calm and need for privacy. These traits produce or fuel his energy and focus for his work.

Cancer does well in careers that provide services, nurture others, improve lives. Cancer is the "whisperer" for horses, infants, and troubled souls.

In his own soul he dreams of developing long-range plans and grand-scale concepts for communities as well as for social improvements. Cancer wants to work for two things: his paycheck and to better mankind. He is not motivated by money alone, although his financial success makes it appear otherwise.

THE CANCER PROFILE

Amniotic ♋ *Tenacious*

Outside of work, Cancer is a clown. He is funny and a pleasant pal. However, in the work arena, he is more demanding—no silliness here. He has a plan, a goal. His primary goal is to make money, lots of it. If other signs can become millionaires, Cancer can become a billionaire.

What does Cancer do on weekends? He visits his mom, and undoubtedly runs into a Capricorn or two doing the same thing.

Cancer reveres his origins and views each generation like a strand of pearls—each ancestor unique, mysteriously linked, and a priceless contributor in his own way to the present. Cancer's love for his family, his parents, his family tree is part of his drive at work and at home.

Cancer often takes cooking classes for recreation. He remodels the house. Or for his time alone, his sacred time, he goes to where nature is most irresistible, on the cliffs overlooking land and sea or off fishing. Cancer may travel to antique trade shows for appraisals on family heirlooms.

With a remarkable love for the ocean, Cancer is amniotic by nature. Helen Keller, the physically challenged and remarkably tenacious scholar, tried to make a crab her pet, for she too loved the ocean that she could only smell and touch. The inhabitants of the sea fascinated her. A primal bond with the waters exists for the Cancer-born.

Dealing well with change, Cancer adapts naturally. Assigning him a series of varied projects will be just fine with him.

In today's business climate, Cancer has certain advantages. Power is shifting from big money and big corporations to the individual with savvy. If the "Industrial Age was about powerful organizations, the new era is about powerful individuals. 'Empowerment' is more than a buzzword—it's a pretty good label for the transfer of authority to self-directed individuals and teams." And, Cancer always excels at self-direction.

Cancer, for all his sensitivity, is a fighter by nature. Remember that as he is at his charming, most gracious self. Cancer is very fit in the survival game, no matter what life deals him. Because of this, you must be very able yourself if you are at cross-purposes with a Cancer.

THE CANCER BOSS

Headed for Success ♋ *Someone Who Hates Deceit*

Cancer has the memory of an elephant, and his management style reflects this. Sympathetic and charitable, he rewards for positive reinforcement. So as you produce within the company, you will be rewarded financially if the Cancer boss has anything to say about it.

Still, it is best not to make a mistake in the value arena. If you fail in the integrity equation, the Cancer has a memory like no other. His heart becomes hard like his shell.

Since the Cancer is so in tune with people's feelings, so able with extrasensory perception, you need to be prepared for the fact that he can, or nearly can, read your mind. You should think twice about this ESP of his.

If you are listening to his instructions and thinking that he needs to lose a few pounds, or that he is being overly concerned about the welfare of someone whose performance has been poor lately, change your thoughts quickly. Think instead of the time he saved your job, remind yourself how he talked you through that painful divorce, and make yourself cozy and receptive.

If you are insincere, if you are disloyal or dishonest and not aboveboard, Cancer will sense it. He can pick up clues in the way you shift your feet, blink your eyes, or put your hands to your mouth. So be careful. He will not tolerate deceit. Cancer bosses can't stand bickering or fussing among the family at work. He is willing to listen, however, to the disgruntled.

If you listen to him, you will hear him talk about family values and compassion. If you watch, you will see him try to be honorable and warm with a touch, a smile, or a gesture.

Cancer wants to see you become a self-starter. Because he is of the entrepreneurial variety or temperament, he wants you to grow in this direction yourself. He has plans for you as his companies merge.

Mergers, a very Cancerian concept, are usually handled differently by the Cancer. Merv Griffin wanted to announce a particular acquisition a few years ago. How does a Cancer announce mergers? Griffin invited a group of fellow art patrons to one of his estates in California, his home. He served hors d'oeuvres and champagne from decks overlooking his private, man-made lake in the middle of the desert. In between singing a few songs by the piano for his guests, he made his announcement. No press release for him.

When Cancer faces opposition at work, he retreats into his shell, his cubbyhole, or perhaps takes a trip to the lake. No sunshine here. When he's gloomy, you know it. He won't try to fake it.

Along the way to success, the Cancer may stumble and fall. He can and does get swept away by his emotions from time to time or tide to tide, and this sometimes gets him into a bit of a mess at work.

So when he takes a magical flight, when he dreams his dreams, let him keep his hope, for just behind his disappointment is his own rainbow and pot of gold. Be staunch in your belief in him. Stand by the Cancer, because his internal compass is headed north.

CANCER SUCCESS STORIES

Steve Forbes was born to the Cancer billions and has taken the helm of the family business.

George Getty set up some little Cancer babies for a lifetime of inheritance.

Estee Lauder, the woman who created the cosmetic line, always thought she was "growing a nice little business." When she first started her firm, she changed her voice as she answered the phone, pretending to be the billing department, shipping department, and so on. The Cancer businessperson can be very folksy.

Merv Griffin, not born with any particular family advantage, has worked his way into a spectacular fortune. Having created family games, he also built spas that stress the experience of pampering and nurturing—a good example of Cancer excelling in the service industry.

The family ties of George W. Bush on both his mother's and father's side, which date back to the Plymouth landing party, surely enhanced the entire future ancestry of the Bushes. George W. Bush has made it clear that he prizes loyalty in people who work for and with him. It could have been said by any Cancer, but George W. said it best when he described his presidential campaign, "We are expanding our base, without destroying our foundations."

Whether the foundation is philosophical or literal, the home base must be preserved by Cancer. Like his career, he builds his home, brick by brick.

OTHER FAMOUS CANCERS

P. T. Barnum	Tom Hanks
James Brolin	Lorrie Morgan
Bill Cosby	Chris O'Donnell
Tom Cruise	Richard Simmons
John Cusack	Carly Simon
Harrison Ford	Ringo Starr
John Glenn	Meryl Streep
Jerry Hall	Vera Wang

RESOURCES

Miner, Margaret, and Hugh Rawson. 1994. *The New International Dictionary of Quotations*. New York: Signet Books.

Peterson, Linda. 2000. "Estee Lauder: Success Never Smelled So Sweet," *Biography* (June).

Pritchett, Price. 1996. *Mind Shift*. Dallas, TX: Pritchett and Associates.

Thorpe, Helen. 2000. "How Bush Became a Brawler," *George* (May).

Tobias, Cynthia Ulrich. 1995. *The Way We Work*. Nashville, TN: Broadman & Holman.

CHAPTER 5

THE RINGMASTER

LEO ■ JULY 23 TO AUGUST 23

HOW TO SPOT A LEO

Creative ♌ *Confident* ♌ *Good at Making an Entrance*

A certain flair is evident in the Leo walk. Each step is a statement, full of drama, striking poses. Leo exudes a hint of the lion or lioness stalking. He possesses a touch of the king or queen, stately and dominating, assessing the kingdom in the air around him. He is not casual or hurried. Leo takes his time, enough time to pause and pose. No one makes an entrance like the Leo.

Leo does not like to be approached casually. He likes appointments, and he likes punctuality on your part—8:07 A.M. is not around eight, but seven minutes after. He is quick, but he does not rush. Leo is rash, but he is not foolish. And, like the cat he is, his eyes have power. Be careful in your approach, and stop to read his eyes first.

The fifth sign of the zodiac, Leo was born to perform, to entertain, and to, well, dazzle us all. Leo lives a gold-card life, has a huge personality, a certain degree of celebrity (even when unfounded), and a will of steel. Leo, a bit impish and enchanting, has a formidable temper and a heart of gold.

Some of Leo's most notable characteristics are his larger-than-life dreams, his playful almost childlike enthusiasms, and his ability

71

to develop and promote his ideas. Leo is impulsive and appears to have boundless energy.

Since the beginning of time, Leo has been living a life of grandeur, pomp, theater, and adventure. Influential friends always come into his world. His imagination and self-confidence often lead him into a life of importance.

Some fields in which Leo excels are: commander in chief or CEO, rock star, department head, child-care worker, lion tamer, stage manager, heart specialist, and jeweler. A few Leos have pseudo careers, romanticized resumes, and a few educational exaggerations. Still, whatever Leo does, he often ends up in creative, influential, star-studded professions.

WHAT DRIVES THE LEO?

Pride ♌ *Self-Esteem Issues*

Leo is proud. His pride drives him. Like other Leo traits, there is a positive and negative side to the lion's ego. While pride may "goeth before a fall," it is also associated with self-esteem and related to success potentials. Often pride helps us to put our best foot forward; pride is behind the expectation to win and the ability to achieve occupational successes.

It is the self-esteem of the Leo salesman that turns every contact into a contract. Why? Because Leo hates to fail. Leo was born to lead and to take charge. He does not relate to small ideas or expectations, and there is nothing petty about Leo.

The more moderate pace and style of the earth signs of Taurus, Virgo, and Capricorn make the Leo feel stalled and weighted down. The Leo, however, finds a facsimile of sorts in the unlimited ambitions of the Capricorn. A Capricorn's desire to reach the top, for recognition and acclaim, is instantly recognized by the canny Leo. For this reason, Capricorn and Leo can accomplish many extraordinary things. But, they cannot be at cross-purposes, which often happens when wills are strong.

The air signs of Gemini, Libra, and Aquarius have much to offer the Leo when it comes to putting Leo creations and inventions into patents, plans, or copyrights. The air signs' talent for taking concepts and placing them into actualities often helps the Leo.

The water signs of Pisces and Cancer provide vision for the sun-ruled center of the zodiac. They offer intuition to the Leo ad agency mentality. They inspire Leo to think things through, beyond the instant. Scorpio often clashes with the Leo and his fiery approach to work styles. Scorpio, a warrior, does not mix well with self-proclaimed royalty.

The fellow fire signs of Aries and Sagittarius reinforce the action words of *initiate, originate,* and *throw-procedure-out-the-window* if necessary to get things rolling. The fire signs are the dynamic trio, equal in enthusiasms. But, they are also in need of a little water or earth to calm them as they ignite with every new brainstorm.

THE LEO WORK STYLE

Fast Paced ♌ *Creative* ♌ *On a Grand Scale*

Gold, the color of his ruler the sun, provides Leo with continuous vitality. Ornate Louis XIV furniture, Versace patterns, knockoffs or not, leather picture frames, Persian rugs, and perks of caviar and a personal stylist were made for the Leo-born. With Neiman Marcus wish books and Christie's Auction House catalogues to surround him, Leo is inspired to work, for Leo loves the accoutrements and acquisitions that work provides.

Leo wants assignments with a lot of options, with the possibility for unique solutions. He does not want too many restrictions and prefers a fast pace. Frequently impatient with any excess of regulations, he likes to be encouraged to do something new. Leo often does his best work when given positive reinforcements and lots of praise, the more lavish the better. You simply cannot flatter the Leo too much. A round of applause is appreciated.

Realize that Leo can get things done. Even if it is not your way or the standard way. Don't take a hard stance. After all, his way is usually a stellar success.

THE LEO STRENGTHS

Creative Intelligence ♌ *Ability to Command*

While many different kinds of intelligence exist, each astrological sign possesses one or more areas in which it is most likely to excel. The Leo has a strong creative intelligence and functions best at this level. Leo, one of the leadership signs, does best when in a position of command.

Leo is the three-year-old drama queen, the ten-year-old lead in the school play, and the twenty-year-old theater student. Leo is sunny, golden, popular, and the first to be noticed in most situations. However, Leo is often addicted to attention and theatrics, and this quality can get him into some situations that compromise his other outstanding qualities.

THE LEO FAVORITE WORK ENVIRONMENT

Surroundings That Offer a Meteoric Rise to the Top
Offices with Glamour or Prestige

Leo loves velvet curtains, klieg lights, spotlights, sunshine, platforms, and podiums. He decorates his office with oranges, reds, and golds all mixed up. When seated near a Leo outside his preferred environment, you might see him struggling with his day job, waiting tables between auditions. Or he may be assigned a cubicle or small workstation that is so beneath his stature that the only clues to the lion's heart are works in progress that clutter his desk or "misplaced" invitations to the season's most prominent social events. Nothing was misplaced, by the way, but calculated to remind you of his stature. If any of that did not get your attention, he will receive calls at work from influential persons of every walk of life. Should you appear obtuse, he will find it necessary to drop names.

Leo usually keeps photos of his children or a group of children he is working with nearby. Leo is excellent with children.

All of this is designed to remind the both of you that he is on the rise no matter how humble his beginnings in life, or with you at work.

When you think of humble beginnings, think of Arnold Schwarzenegger coming from Austria with his movie-star fantasies attracting him to America and its newness. And, yes, its richness. Arnold is a powerhouse, an inspiration, and as he calls himself, a "driven machine." He desired fame, dreamed of fame, and climbed from Mr. Universe to a megastar.

THE LEO EMPLOYEE/COWORKER

Popular and Inspiring ♌ *Happiest with a Title* ♌ *Adept at Negotiation*

Leo is popular. Before long you realize that he has met just about everyone of any importance in some field and frequented the trendiest places. He is an excellent conversationalist; you won't even care whether or not he tells you the truth. He is, above all, entertaining.

Leo loves the finest and best. Europe, especially places like Italy, attracts him like flies to the blue light. If his job is too mundane, he will create another eight hours a day for party time, networking time, Toastmasters, or local college auditions. It doesn't matter what so much as that he is performing at some level with the lights shining over his head.

Leo cures office morale problems with his own motivational lectures. He is a one-man cheerleading section for the company.

Leo, for all his positive attributes, can be the ringleader for rebellion as well. This usually comes as a result of his need for constant stimulation and challenge at work. He facilitates trouble when monotony sets in. Defiance can also be his reaction to his need to question authority.

Leo inspires other workers with his presence; he excels at mentoring. His determination demonstrates that where there is a will, there really is a way. Leo shows that poor is the person who has no dreams, for it is the richness of Leo's dreams that nourishes his coworkers.

Leo is adept at the art of negotiation. He is generous with cost of living increases, as he truly understands cost of living. Luxury items are a near necessity for the Leo-born. He will go to great lengths to see that his fellow workers get step increases or whatever the company offers. He is not stingy.

No one loves a title more than Leo. Because of this, he encourages the company in creative ways to offer titles to enhance company images. Vice president of fact finding, manager of profit assessment, or similar vague titles often help appease the overworked and underpaid.

Leos usually end up with great titles. Elizabeth Dole started out as May Queen, became the president of American Red Cross, and ran for the office of president of the United States.

Another dubbed queen was the queen of Camelot, Jacqueline Kennedy Onassis. When working as an editor in New York, Jacqueline received a reply from Frank Sinatra declining her offer to have his autobiography written. He sent her flowers and a card that read,

"You are America's Queen. God bless you, always. Love, Frank." It is always easier to deny a Leo's request by accompanying the denial with a note of praise and an extravagant gesture.

If you are working with a Leo and he does not yet have his kingship, make sure you acknowledge his royalty by at least a nickname. Otherwise, he will be insulted. You will be stepping on his big paws, which is not a wise thing to do.

THE LEO LEARNING STYLE

Concrete/Random ♌ *Experimental* ♌ *Innovative*

The way a Leo learns, or the way in which his mind works, is considered concrete when viewed in the context of the Gregorc Model of Learning Styles.

Everyone and every sign observe the same sights and sounds, yet each perceives them in different ways. While at some level we all see what we want to see, we still convert information in two distinct fashions. One perceptual quality of the Leo is his concrete learning style.

When you think or perceive in a concrete way, you register the world around you via the five senses: touch, sight, smell, taste, and hearing. Leo loves to make his ideas and fantasies a reality. This is how he converts his innovations into a physical condition. The Leo can take an idea for a play and write it out from scenes in his head. He sees it all before it hits the paper. But, after it is written, he reinforces his work via his five senses. He improves on the visuals: how it will be viewed, what musical score to accompany it, what lighting to enhance the scenes, etc.

When you present a project or proposal to a Leo, remember to appeal to his sense of drama and his need for concrete demonstrations. Consider lighting, sounds, and smells to enhance his vision of the work. Leo makes no attempt to read your mind, but he can see the big picture with a little sensory stimulation. And he wants the information now. He is not good at waiting and long pauses unless he is posing.

While all of us process information from both a concrete and an abstract viewpoint, we have a preference. This preference is where we are most comfortable in learning and working situations. Leo wants a direct presentation, no subtleties, no walks around the park in dialogue.

The second component to learning is how we order our information. The Leo prefers unstructured, quick methods of organizing, and this intelligence preference is a random learning style. The Leo learns better when he is given a chance to think of possibilities, to satisfy his natural curiosity with explanations. Leos also learn better when they feel they are in control of the situation to a large degree.

Leos are the ones to fight for a principle. For example, other signs may give in and do what is necessary to survive within a corporation, but the Leo will fight over small or large issues to prove a point. In fact, he will quit his job over an issue if pushed.

One Leo I know was excelling at work; success was written all over her reviews. However, the company had a rule, an issue over dress or appropriate attire, that the Leo did not agree with. Management issued an either/or ultimatum. Well, her eyes took on a peculiar green glow, and she said something to the effect that it would be "or" and quit on the spot. No fuss or regrets. If you issue the Leo an ultimatum, you had better be ready for the consequences. When working with the Leo, remember these needs are part of his work style. Approach him with the positive, encourage spontaneity, give him something to feel proud about, and he will be as tame as your Aunt Martha's old tabby cat.

THE BEST WAY FOR A LEO TO LEARN

Role-Playing ♌ *Enthusiastically Inspired by Supervisors*

Leo learns well from role-playing. Let him actively participate in everything from training sessions to hands-on work instructions. Make work and learning an adventure. Encourage excitement in the way projects and changes are presented, such as, "Hey, your last report was such a knockout we are asking you to do another for next month." Make it sound exciting. Enthusiasm charges the Leo.

For all of Leo's fire and impulse, he does not embrace change as easily as the other fire signs of Aries and Sagittarius. In fact, Leo can be slow to adapt to newer methods unless he initiates them. Just because a rule changes doesn't mean Leo will accept it without challenge.

One Leo recently was advised how to prepare a proposal with a new "winning format." She knew that the old one she had been using was no longer working. It was good, but not good enough to win sales anymore. Still, her Leo pride got in the way of accepting necessary change. This is what I mean about the two sides of Leo's pride. You need to work with Leo on this when you see him having difficulty accepting change.

THE LEO INTELLIGENCE

Creative ♌ *Learns Best from Trial and Error* ♌ *Quick to Learn*

Howard Gardner, Harvard professor and prominent researcher, developed the theory that many different kinds of intelligence exist. He identified at least seven while other theories are speculative.

Recently, emotional intelligence has been suggested as another form of IQ. Daniel Goleman's work on this has opened our eyes in the West to the possibility of genius beyond more traditional measures. The importance of the varieties of mental capacities, or ways to be smart, may reflect the passions that incline us toward our work.

The Leo type of intelligence is creative. Creative intelligence is similar to emotional intelligence in that traditional methods of testing have ignored the importance of the ability to create fresh new concepts and the power of imagination.

Creative IQ may be considered part of what shapes Leo's success at work. Leo has a high level of energy as well as a vivid imagination. This skill begins as a child when a twig becomes a magical wand. Later this creative bent takes a new look at a familiar can of tomato soup and turns it into a work of art. Andy Warhol of the strobe-lit '70s who created the silver Elvis and the multicolored Marilyn demonstrates the extraordinary ability to revisualize for the sake of art.

Warhol said that he wanted "to invent a new kind of fast food . . . a waffle thing that had the food on one side and the drink on the other—like ham and Coke." Needless to say, Leo does not always hit a home run with every idea, but he is certainly entertaining.

Any Leo worth his salt stood up and roared when Nuala Beck, author of *Shifting Gears: Thriving in the New Economy*, said that "more Americans work in the movie industry than the automotive industry." How thrilling this is for the Leo, born to theatrics, the magic of moviemaking, and the grand theater. At last, enough job openings for the Leo.

Give Leo space; allow him to clutter, to place objects upside down, and to make order from his chaos. It is thought that people who prefer to work in chaos are trying on a daily basis to make order of things and reinforce their belief in themselves and their power over situations. Leo needs to feel in control in many different ways.

Make sure he has good lighting, as Leo always looks for some lighting to set off his wayward locks and give him proper backdrop.

When preparing training sessions for the Leo, acknowledge him frequently with eye contact and approving nods; let him offer suggestions. Quick to learn, Leo doesn't need a lot of repetition as a rule. The sign on his door should read Department of Winging It, for Leo learns best from trial and error.

When working with Leo, remember that his learning style is concrete and random. Leo is also of the fire element and the fixed mode astrologically. The fixed type is inclined to resist a lot of changes unless, of course, they originate from him.

The Leo profile includes his need to produce, lead, inspire, be in charge, and quite frankly to self-promote. This talent, when extended to the company or organization, can be a valuable asset for the group as a whole.

Leo is definitely, predominately, and unabashedly an extroverted vocational type. Leo lives in the moment, every exhilarating second of the day. While he can see long-range effects and plans from his work, he does not want to deal with the details of the mundane.

Leo does well in any career that requires energy and enthusiasm. He excels in sales and can get his foot in almost any door.

Fact-finding missions are of little interest to the Leo unless he is pursuing something creative, such as how to get the waffle on the other side of the cola in his food brainstorm.

He receives instructions best when they sound challenging, are open-ended, and allow him to carve his own initials on his work. Leo likes to work where he feels appreciated and frequently applauded. He likes to imagine that there is theater in the dullest of jobs and wants to hear some murmur from the crowd. He was born with greasepaint in his blood.

THE LEO BOSS

Good at Delegating ♌ Driven ♌ Tough

The Leo boss will chatter the entire time he is reorganizing the corporation and delegating the hundreds of tasks he can conjure up in a forty-hour week. The Leo boss needs someone who will listen to his every word, smile approvingly, and work like he has a hurricane heading his way. Because the Leo boss is a human tornado at work when inspired, he has an awesome, powerful force behind him.

It shouldn't surprise you then that the Leo boss doesn't want to see any stifled yawns from his employees. Nor does he want to see a slight curve of the lips as he makes an absurd statement or unfounded assumption. You simply must believe in him. You must do this because, for some strange reason and for all his considerable vanity, Leo does possess some insecurities and doubts about his abilities. He would blush at the mere mention of this, so when you read this about him, keep it to yourself. It could make the difference in your future employability.

Leo often makes some real blunders in his career. Let's consider the advertising executive who makes an error in slogans for overseas accounts. One individual, and there was undoubtedly a Leo along the way in this misadventure, did not realize that the slogan for Kentucky Fried Chicken, "Finger lickin' good" in the United States, became "Eat your fingers off" in China. This is the kind of error a Leo makes when he jumps into the ad campaign, annual report, or sales presentation without checking the facts.

When Leo faces opposition or disappointment at work, you will see the courage of the lion firsthand. Think of Jacqueline Kennedy Onassis and the enormity of her courage and strength at her lowest moments. Leo is tougher than the rest of us can ever imagine. Whether with the little girl voice of Onassis or the roar of Mick Jagger, the Leo is one of the toughest people you will ever meet.

Leo sells dreams. He only asks that you believe in his dreams and put forth boundless energies to help him pursue each new vision.

Leo is not above taking your ideas and claiming them for his own. He does not consider this theft, because he has a way of believing that he was the catalyst for your idea. Without him, you would never have come up with much on your own. Remember, Leo's frame of mind was born from a perceived state of royalty.

LEO SUCCESS STORIES

Like many Leos, Napoleon Bonaparte had a fascination with Italy. His ambitions were boundless. He had himself proclaimed the emperor of the French. At the ceremony, he took his crown from the hands of Pope Pius VII and proceeded to set it on his own head.

Napoleon I became the master of Europe after nearly rearranging the continent. He named his family members as co-throners. And when his reign was at an end, he had to be forced to retreat. President William Jefferson Clinton had no intention of resigning from the White House after he was impeached. Leo hates to relinquish power.

Napoleon's legends were always popular in his birthplace of France. He mesmerized followers and romanticized all that he accomplished. But, while he was ruthless, he was also generous to his enemies. This twisted ruthless-generous conflict much like

Napoleon's is part of every Leo dilemma. Leo shows no pity on the rise, but once his considerable ambitions are satisfied, he can be beneficent. However, by then he has often generated a fair amount of animosity.

Napoleon Bonaparte said, "If you want a thing done well, do it yourself." He considered that leaders are really leaders in hope. Unstoppable, enthusiastic Leo radiates hope.

Before the years of equality, when women had to hide their considerable light under bushels, Leo women rose to power in more nontraditional ways. A few great courtesans were born under the sign of Leo. One of them, Madame DuBarry, had a fictionalized marriage to her lover's brother in order to be with the king. Knowing Leo, she no doubt used her power with the king to facilitate her own dreams and desire for authority.

Remember, too, there is always some fictionalizing with the ambitious Leo. Most Leos do not go to these extremes of pseudo or near fact, however.

Fiction-based situations or not, as with DuBarry, great marketing and continuous reinvention as with Madonna, Leo is born to be the king or queen of whatever he or she pursues.

Another formidable Leo success was Henry Ford. After disagreement with his first organization and early associates, he formed Ford Motor Company. Four years later he bought the stocks from his associates and kept the money in the family.

Ford, famous for paying wages far beyond the average of the times, also was generous with profit sharing. He had a paternalistic attitude toward his employees. His career was peppered with antagonisms, disputes, and heated arguments. Yet he emerged, renowned and successful.

Perhaps the Leo is best expressed by Ford's personal bottom line: "He can who thinks he can, and he can't who thinks he can't. This is an inexorable, indisputable law."

♋

OTHER FAMOUS LEOS

Ben Affleck
Rosanna Arquette
Halle Berry
Sandra Bullock
Vivica A. Fox
Iman
Peter Jennings
Lisa Kudrow

Jennifer Lopez
The Queen Mother
 of England
Pete Sampras
Stephanie Seymour
Wesley Snipes
Danielle Steel

RESOURCES

Anderson, Christopher. 1998. *Jackie After Jack: Portrait of the Lady*. New York: William Morrow and Company.

Beck, Nuala. 1995. *Shifting Gears: Thriving in the New Economy*. New York: Harper Collins Canada, U.S. Edition.

Bridgewater, William, and Seymour Kurtz, eds. 1963. *The Illustrated Columbia Encyclopedia*. New York: Columbia University Press.

Dunkel, Tom. 1999. "Millennium Man," *George* (November).

Hackett, Pat, ed. 1989. *The Andy Warhol Diaries*. New York: Time Warner.

Miner, Margaret, and Hugh Rawson. 1994. *The New International Dictionary of Quotations*. New York: Signet Books.

CHAPTER 6

THE REFORMER

VIRGO ▪ AUGUST 23 TO SEPTEMBER 23

HOW TO SPOT A VIRGO

Dependable ♍ *Measured* ♍ *Able to Transform Elements*

Virgo is the workhorse of the zodiac. He loves the outdoors and exercise, but he tends to look anxiously around (does he need blinders?), take a step, and wonder if the ground is even. For if it is not, he could suffer a slight maladjustment to his spine. The Virgo is a mental machine. His pace is uneasy, his walk mechanical. He is not concerned about making an appearance or entrance; he just doesn't want to suffer falls or injuries in the process. And more often than not, wherever he goes, he will get there a little early.

Virgo is usually slender and wiry. But never be fooled; he is sturdy and as solid as the earth. This very sturdiness will take him to the chairmanship of Bell Labs, the editorship of *The New Yorker*, the publisher of *Scientific American*, CEO of Ford Motors, or the president of Coca-Cola, to name a few.

Virgo would never throw out instructions. Indeed, he is more inclined to highlight passages from all manuals and materials he deems important. From day one, Virgo is notably serious about his position and its job description. Virgo is a measured person, and he is precise in his approach to his work.

Some of Virgo's most notable characteristics are that he is methodical, sincere, and dependable, and he has a clear-cut way of presenting ideas. While he is deliberate and does not make instant assessments, he is not slow. He is appraising. A creature of habit, his mind must adjust to change before his body can. Imagine a Virgo jumping from any business cliff without having surveyed, plotted, and calculated the terrain long before he spoke a word or took a step. Leaps of any sort do not come naturally for the Virgo.

Virgo often finds himself in fields that require transformation. He sees ways to utilize the bubbling hot water of the mineral springs or the pharmacological potentials of the outdoors. He is the faith healer, medical visionary, masseuse, herbalist, bearded mystic, and ultimate social worker of his time.

Virgo has been involved in religious crusades and quests of one kind or another since the beginning of mankind. He heals not with metal but with his hands and heart. Virgo is the first to know that health begins in the mind, then in the body.

Virgo is not afraid to be a humble servant of the earth, for in this service he can watch the budding flower and the erupting volcanoes. When Virgo is out of the flow of energies involved in services to others, he can become faultfinding, arrogant, and fearful.

Just when you think that he is some throwback of the '60s, the Virgo lands one of the most prestigious jobs in the country. For all his appreciation of the earth and nature, he is a natural-born worker and his corporate ethics take him far in the business community.

WHAT DRIVES THE VIRGO?

Crusades ♍ *Facts*

Virgo is driven by natural curiosity. He wants to know how and why, not to mention when and where. He is excited by fact in the same way others are excited by fiction, possibilities, or what ifs.

Virgo chips away at the facts until every nit is picked and every hair is split. That is how he approaches anything that interests him.

The slower pace of his fellow earth signs, Taurus and Capricorn, make Virgo feel cozy and comforted. He finds himself in sync with their earthy approach to situations. The practicality of the three signs bonds Virgo.

The air signs of Gemini, Libra, and Aquarius share some of Virgo's passion for discovery and exploration. And, while they analyze well with Virgo, they do not possess the same intensity of commitment and conformance and detail that is so important to the Virgo-born.

The fire signs add impetus to Virgo's zeal. Fire and earth are steamrollers, and together they get it done. The Aries, Leo, and Sagittarius can speak, dramatize, and publicize the Virgo mechanics. Virgo needs the excitement the fire signs generate to have others share his vision.

The water signs of Cancer, Scorpio, and Pisces could add some intuitive steps to the Virgo scientific approach to all matters. But, Virgo shares little regard for things outside the database. Pisces, however, shares Virgo's love of the mystical, the spiritual, and the redemptive quests.

THE VIRGO WORK STYLE

Focused ♍ *Detail Oriented* ♍ *Able to See What Others Miss*

You will not be amazed to learn by now that it is rare to find a Virgo who is not meticulous and structured. Most Virgos start out in childhood sorting the Halloween candy by brand, color, or size. By the time a Virgo reaches adulthood and an office setting, he is easily recognized by his arrangement of paper clips by new and used, large and small.

Virgo likes an office that is clean and efficient, with cabinets for his medicines and personal effects. He likes metals and clean lines. Modern versus retro appeals to him. Often he is nurturing something—a sickly plant among an array of healthy, green ferns and philodendron. He is attracted to the color blue; perhaps it reminds him of the great outdoors. Virgo is adaptable and can work well in a structured indoor environment, but in his compulsive heart he yearns to be near mountains and pine trees. Ah, to set up office in Sequoia National Park.

Continuous changes in plans and strategies or too many new challenges to deal with fray the ragged nerves of the Virgo. A hundred years ago everyone called these nervous tics hissies, tissies, and vapors. Today they are temporary breakdowns and panic disorders brought on by interruptions.

Focused, Virgo is distracted from his path by thirty phone calls and three unexpected staff meetings. For, in his concentration, he sees what others have missed. He sees every tree in the forest, and your conflicting needs or assignments detour him.

THE VIRGO STRENGTHS

Spatial Intelligence ♍ *Transforms and Restructures*

While many different kinds of intelligence exist, all astrological signs possess one or more areas in which they are most likely to excel. No one type of intelligence makes one or the other more noteworthy or important. Each type of intelligence has its own wonder and brings the rest of us its special gift.

The mental Virgo functions best at a spatial level. Because of this, Virgo can restructure or transform (reform, as well) situations and structures.

Virgo, who loves to work with his hands, is a craft person. He can spot the relationship in patterns and designs that others miss.

He has a natural sense of balance and symmetry. This helps him tremendously in traditional IQ test scores.

Since he can use spatial intelligence to re-create things visually, it is not surprising that Virgo receives instructions and images rather quickly. Part of his inherent gift is the ability to nearly photograph an image in his mind. Because of this, Virgo is often perceived as tediously smarter than the rest of us. Virgo excels in mechanical fields such as architecture, drafting, and engineering, which are naturals for him. Still, he is often lured from these fields for the more emotional pursuits of earth and healing. While Virgo is precise in his emotional expressions, there is a certain magic in his heart that will not be denied.

THE VIRGO FAVORITE WORK ENVIRONMENT

Outdoors ♍ Work That Requires Stamina

Virgo loves outdoors, but will work patiently indoors. He can be found anywhere hard work is required. He shirks from nothing.

In the newsletter "Hiring the Best," it is reported that companies are screening employees for the "intensity" trait. This trait, like stamina, persistence, and determination, is one every employer wants to see.

The intensity trait refers to someone who has a tendency to be a workaholic. Employees who will put in whatever hours are needed to get the job done, like Virgo, are a dream. Or so it would seem. Yet, employers find that this can lead to burnout, feeling overworked and overwhelmed. It also leads to a loss of creativity. Some companies are taking action to give the driven employee the break they will not take for themselves. S. C. Johnson & Son, Inc., posts signs that say, "Room Sealed by Order of 'No Meeting Day' Police." The idea is to help the more compulsive workers to get the time for rest and renewal they need. This is perfect for Virgo.

THE VIRGO EMPLOYEE/COWORKER

Is Inclined to Nervousness ♍ *Is Ruled by Habit* ♍ *Has a Cause*

The witty Virgo is a word master. When Virgo, with his perfect hair and pristine clothing, does his stand-up routines, it may appear incongruous to anyone watching. Perhaps, too, this is part of why he is so funny. His humor is often self-deprecating.

Virgo is an odd creature with plenty of quirks. And, yes, he is a health phobic. Let me share a Virgo coworker story with you to illustrate.

This Virgo was talking to me one day, freshly showered (he admits to taking several a day) and looking for the world like a page from *GQ*. He was planning a letter-writing campaign to Congress to pass a law to help eliminate germs in public buildings by adding a second doorknob to the doors. This way he figured we could diminish the concentration of germs in public buildings as well as in private offices.

While this may seem totally obsessive-compulsive to the rest of us, Virgo has made sanitary contributions before. John Howard was a British reformer and his issues about human circumstances were for improved sanitary conditions and health care in prisons. Howard became part of a system of rehabilitation through both his work and his religious teachings in prison reform. How very Virgo.

Virgo is the redeemer; he always wants to heal, rehabilitate, and reform. He wants to save us all. Virgo has a cause, and even if it is just to keep the weeds out of his garden on the weekends, he is diligent about it.

How does Virgo have fun then? He fuses glass, grows herbs, makes pottery, and dreams of going to the Nova Scotia College of Art and Design. He makes plans for planting a small garden down some quaint road. He is a simple person with many complexities.

The Virgo cure for office dissension and conflict is to break it down, to investigate each and every complaint. He will agonize over each person's problems, hurts, and embarrassments. Then he will come to a conclusion and bluntly assess the situation. He will be critical and often horrifyingly accurate. It is chilling to watch the colder side of the Mercury-ruled.

It is worth noting that Virgo is a very determined sign. While he does not set out to lead or promote himself, he often ends up at the head of something, often after a long, winding path of just plain old hands-on hard work.

Virgo is deliberate. He is not impulsive, grandiose, or speculative in his work or career. But he can weather adversity and great personal trials and tribulations if necessary to win his objective. He believes that when he works twelve hours a day, seven days a week, he will get his lucky break.

An example of the working style of Virgo on a mission is the late Margaret Sanger. She began her career as a nurse, and her work among the poor convinced her of the need for information concerning contraception. Only problem was that it was not legal to publish this information for distribution.

In her zeal, she published *The Woman Rebel* and was indicted for attacking legislative restrictions on birth control. After a few other birth control issues brought her some jail time, she finally won an appeal. This appeal paved the way for doctors to form birth control organizations and give advice and information in New York. Sanger formed several birth control organizations and helped redeem a social and medical issue of enormous importance.

Virgo is a radical, somewhat of a zealot, and without him many would lack the courage to take on some of the more difficult issues of the human condition. Because of his intensity when driven by the gods of social issues and reform, he works himself into near exhaustion. When not compelled about an issue or situation, he can be the first to relax and just enjoy the fruits of the earth.

Next time you think Virgo is possessed, remember that there have been several Virgo saints, not to mention the good deeds of Mother Teresa of Calcutta and her inspired work for the sick and dying.

THE VIRGO LEARNING STYLE

Structured ♍ *Likes Role Models* ♍ *Takes Things Literally*

The way a Virgo learns or the way in which his mind works is considered concrete when viewed in the context of the Gregorc Model of Learning Styles.

Everyone and every sign observe the same sights and sounds, yet each perceives them in different ways. While at some level we all see what we want to see, we still convert information in two distinct fashions. One perceptual quality is a concrete learning style.

When you think or perceive in a concrete way, you need to register the world around you in specific, consistent ways. Concrete perception is reinforced by repetition, numbers, and precise instructions. Virgo takes things literally; what he sees and hears is reality for him.

For example, Virgo needs to see the practical side of things. He is not attracted to the fanciful or half-baked. Virgo says what he means and means what he says and will assume that you are doing the same. This is his special language.

Virgo excels at keeping appointments and schedules and maintaining systems. Unlike his counterparts in the office, when he networks he carefully and systematically files the business cards that he has accumulated. "Let's do lunch" is a commitment, not a phrase.

Virgo is not interested in subtleties. If you want something from him, ask him. He will give you a yes or no. Virgo is not long-winded.

While all of us process information from both a concrete and an abstract viewpoint, we have a preference. This preference is where we are most comfortable in learning and working situations. Virgo is comfortable with structure and role models.

The second component to learning is how we order our information. Virgo prefers a sequential style of ordering information and learning. He prefers to do things the same way and develops habits quickly. He wants to know what is expected from him. He thinks more of things and data than of individuals. He is not afraid to ask how to do something before he attempts a project.

When Virgo gets a demand to set up new organizational charts, he will not ask why the request was made. He will not bother to wonder who is and is not on the new chart; he will just make up the new chart. You can count on it.

If you want to work with or for a Virgo, remember he has a concrete/sequential learning style and a spatial personality. Of the earth element and the mutable mode astrologically, Virgo is less inclined to be a natural leader, preferring instead to do his own thing.

THE BEST WAY FOR A VIRGO TO LEARN

No Risk-Taking Is Involved ภฦ *Instructions Are Explicit*

Virgo likes to work in quiet; noise is a distraction that he finds taxing. He loves research. Virgo cannot get enough data and information. Because of this, his timing is often off. He may delay decisions until more facts are in and in doing so make the wrong decision of "no decision."

Virgo, while savvy with technology, is not of the dot.com, millionaire, risk-taking breed. Virgo prefers to make decisions based on more than your word for it or your feelings about a project. Virgo will not usually say what he thinks until he is certain of it.

Virgo rarely gets bored as he excels at nearly endless exploration. He excels at tasks that require intense concentration. Remember that as you hand over the plutonium formulations.

THE VIRGO PROFILE

Value-Driven ♍ *Perfectionist*

The basic nature of Virgo fits so closely to the principles of a successful business that it is no wonder that Virgo will make the eventual rise to a capacity of importance in whatever field he chooses.

In the book *In Search of Excellence: Lessons from America's Best-Run Companies*, the authors analyzed excellence in business. They found, among other factors for success, a well-defined set of beliefs and values. These values were relayed not by written guidelines but by telling stories about success and reworking the human nature of its employees to embody these values.

Most of these companies stress qualitative rather than quantitative values. America's best-run companies believe that profit comes as a result of doing something well, rather than profit for profit motives.

Virgo embodies the sound business principles of doing things for the right reason, to provide a needed service, to create the highest quality. He is a natural fit for companies that are about the higher standard. Virgo needs to be in the right value fit to rework, reform, and transform. Without it, he can be overlooked and underappreciated.

Because Virgo is a mental sign, he will do his best work for you when things are spelled out clearly. Write job descriptions and qualifications completely. Get off to a good start.

Give him a chance to mimic tasks with hands-on training and role modeling. Tap into his passion to succeed. Allow him his remoteness, and don't expect his charisma to burst forth on day one. Give him time to thoroughly test his projects. Don't interrupt him needlessly. Give him a clear-cut schedule.

The best of Virgo is waiting untapped for the right company or employer. He won't jump right in like the Aries or promote himself like the Leo, but he will be there to work like the devil for you. Allow his worth to be developed. Just because he is no ball of fire doesn't mean he has no spark.

THE VIRGO BOSS

Is Exacting ♍ *Critiques Performances* ♍ *Doesn't Like Excuses*

Virgo will be in the office early, so don't plan on sneaking in the door at 8:02 A.M. He will expect you to be prepared, so no excuses such as my dog ate my case notes. And, he will be watching you intently, ready to critique.

A Virgo boss sets clear boundaries. You will know what is expected of you, so overflowing notebooks, sloppy grammar, inopportune moments from your last staff meeting will not be passed over the second time around.

Virgo is not a curmudgeon, but he does have certain expectations of everyone. He won't spout off right then and there. He is more likely to internalize his temper tantrums, resulting in a stomachache later in the day for him. But, he will remember your small sins of omission.

You can poke around and move at a snail's pace at work, and he will hardly notice. Virgo's issues are not with speed, or time, or pizzazz, but with solutions and solid performances. His only concern is that your work when presented to him is on the mark, correct, and well thought out.

His compulsive tendencies sometimes get in the way of personal happiness. When overtaxed or unhappy, Virgo starts picking at his perfect cuticle, becomes less tidy, agonizes over past mistakes, slides into depression. A person in a fog, gloomy and unhappy, cannot make his usual astute business decisions.

This is when you can redeem the redeemer, save the savior, and bring in something to be nurtured—a sick plant, broken pottery, a failing grassroots project. Remind Virgo to get out, putter around, look around the forest for the forest.

VIRGO SUCCESS STORIES

Virgo is one of the least self-promoting individuals of the zodiac. Because of this, a lot of success stories have rather unrecognizable names. Virgo wants it that way. Publicity and fanfare would only disrupt him and his work. Nobel Peace Prize–winning Jane Addams wrote *Democracy and Social Ethics*. Loren Eiseley, the anthropologist and environmentalist, wrote seven books on human evolution themes. One of the greatest businessmen of this century, Milton S. Hershey, the candy maker, typified many of the Virgo characteristics, including a tendency to be a bit eccentric but in a wonderful way, of course.

Hershey was a bit of a dreamer in business or so it seemed. His quirks by all accounts included a desire to create a company that was part dream or a bit of heaven here on earth. In the end, after he had amassed a fortune, he gave it all away to his foundations.

Hershey had only a fourth-grade education. Remember, the Virgo-born has an innate ability for intelligence. Hershey failed along his path to success as most successful people do. He made it a point to tell people that failure was a necessary part of life.

President William Howard Taft, like many Virgos, seemed to not get much attention, acclaim, or credit for his efforts. Still, he accomplished much in the White House. Did he do anything for reform? The answer is yes. He did much to improve the social condition of the people of the Philippines.

When asked the secret of his success, Taft replied he always had his "plate the right side up when offices were falling." It is a little like the Virgo who tells you he always gets lucky when he works twelve hours a day, seven days a week. Virgo is simply not boastful in spite of the enormity of his success.

Three Virgo-born saints and two football coaches, Bear Bryant and Tom Landry, prove that Virgos can interact with others, that they are all too human like the rest of the more emotive of us. Virgo just expresses himself as well as his work and success in a more restrained manner.

♍

OTHER FAMOUS VIRGOS

Sean Connery	Sophia Loren
Harry Connick Jr.	Keanu Reeves
Cameron Diaz	Harland Sanders
Hugh Grant	William Saroyan
Buddy Holly	Claudia Schiffer
Lyndon Johnson	Oliver Stone
Tommy Lee Jones	Shania Twain
Stephen King	Trisha Yearwood

RESOURCES

Miner, Margaret, and Hugh Rawson. 1994. *The New International Dictionary of Quotations*. New York: Signet Books.

Peters, Thomas J., and Robert Waterman. 1992. *In Search of Excellence: Lessons from America's Best-Run Companies*. New York: Warner Books.

PART TWO

THE LAST SIX SIGNS

The final six signs of the zodiac begin with Libra, and isn't it just like the Libra to introduce the relationship of all matters? I can't familiarize you with Libra without telling you about how we all work together and how even opposites contain something that reminds us of the other. I feel like Libra is making a speech, standing on top of my word processor all dimpled and darling, before I get to write about him.

In this book, just like in life, Libra would have to head the department of mergers or human resources because Libra represents the hour of day that the sun sets and day blends with mysterious night.

In the zodiac this integration is more than symbolic because the energies work in a different way from the metaphorical night and figurative day. And, it is Libra who reminds us that each of us needs to work together, not pull apart.

Sun signs become harmonious together in mysterious ways. One sun sign speaks and the other thinks, one writes and the other publishes, or one is the voice and one is the voice of reason.

Alchemists claim that it is the opposites that have to be brought together to make one whole. Astrologers believe that either the same or opposite energies can be part of the one complete or whole energy.

The last six sun signs take the original concepts of the first six and put a universal spin on them. These final six signs are the most visible, get the most press (except for that irrepressible Leo energy that challenges the laws of probability), and are able to "partner" energies.

Libra wants us to all get along; Scorpio wants us to pool our monies; Sagittarius wants to unite tribes and get that global business going; Capricorn wants to set the examples; Aquarius wants to do the right thing by everybody; and Pisces, well, if the other signs are a chapter, the Pisces is a book. Pisces wants us to tap into the spiritual realms.

If Libra were to run the personnel department, the problems would flow in an order similar to this:

> Good morning. Gemini, I understand you need that ad copy translated for international markets. You need to check with Sagittarius for all interpretations and overseas matters. And please tell Cancer that Capricorn is having some work-related problems on the home front—something about an accusation of being a workaholic. A little insight should help, and I thought of Cancer.

And so it goes; in our opposite energies we sometimes find the answer to our work-related dilemmas. Maybe we need to look at things from a whole different viewpoint just to open our minds a bit when they close from time to time.

But for now, in the following chapters you will see some of the energies reinforcing the others. It will be subtle but look for it. For herein lies the harmony of the different kinds of intelligence, the different work styles, and the potential for alchemy.

CHAPTER 7

THE PEACEMAKER

LIBRA ▪ SEPTEMBER 23 TO OCTOBER 23

HOW TO SPOT A LIBRA

The Peacemaker ♎ *Calming* ♎ *Able to Manipulate Situations*

Libra glides around, light of foot, in vintage clothes or something equally divine, looking superb. Always coy, Libra walks with a peek-a-boo, flirtatious sway that is attractive regardless how subtle.

Libra moves gracefully, maneuvering crowds and landing next to the most inaccessible, impossible person in the room, and makes a new friend. Libra is as lighthearted as his walk. In the same blithe way, Libra makes his entrance to any profession, and success follows like his bliss.

Libra has an innate charm that is often irresistible coupled with a knack for getting just about whatever it is he wants. It happens naturally, for Libra is winsome, full of grace, and as the saying goes, fair of face. In his personal life and his business life, things flow his way. Because of this, Libra is often an early success without some of the darker days and trying upward paths of other signs.

Libra may review personnel guidelines and job descriptions with an abstract curiosity, as if they do not apply to him at all. Many times they will not be relevant, for Libra can create the exception to every rule.

One of Libra's most notable characteristics is that he is totally charming and will have everyone paying homage within days of his employment. And so begins his career of knowing the right people, picking the right projects, and having that element of good luck that always enters into any final success equation.

Libra frequently lands in careers involving the arts as a model, interior decorator, fashion designer, curator, or artist. He is also excellent in departments of human resources or departments of justice, as a lawyer or paralegal.

Whatever field Libra ends up in, he will be the manipulator, arbitrator, and deal maker. Lee Iacocca was the deal maker in the automotive industry; President Carter and Jesse Jackson have been the negotiators in famous international meetings for peace.

Libra's talents tend toward cautious, conservative approaches. He usually does not offer new or sweeping changes or solutions. He is often vague about how he hopes to accomplish his goals. Libra is likable and most often partners up for success.

Since the beginning of time, Libra has been involved in merging with others. He resolves disputes, smooths troubled waters, paves the way for new ventures, and makes peace for troubled times in any situation.

WHAT DRIVES THE LIBRA?

Relationships ⚖ *Interactions with People*

Relationships drive the Libra. He needs interaction with people; he does not like to work alone. Libra is also driven by curiosity and the need to create harmony in his life and the lives of others.

John Lennon's song "Imagine" could be the theme song for Libra. Gandhi, nearly a mantra, is one associated with the word peace. Both Libras campaigned for armistice during their lives.

The plodding pace of the earth signs, their focus on the material and physical, seems tedious to Libra. Libra knows only the search for conditions such as happiness and personal satisfaction. Taurus is the most easily understood of the earth signs because both Taurus and Libra are creature-comfort driven. Both use their senses rather than their judgments frequently.

The fellow air signs of Gemini and Aquarius communicate well with Libra. Libra understands nonlinear thinking and requires cooperation and alliances. President Dwight Eisenhower worked well with General MacArthur, an Aquarian, who saw and understood the enormity of Eisenhower's success potential early in Eisenhower's career.

The fire signs of Aries, Leo, and Sagittarius work well with Libra. Sagittarius understands Libra's fascination for uniting internal structures and community structures. For all their ability to work well together, Leo is often too ruthless in his methods and ambitions for Libra. Libra Iacocca was taken totally by surprise by the cool and sudden dismissal by Ford, a Leo-created business.

The water signs of Cancer, Scorpio, and Pisces often inspire Libra with their strong, intuitive powers. Libra can approach the water signs for insights the Libra can understand because they come from the gut. Libra's insights come from the heart. Libra is feeling-based and understands decisions involving emotions.

THE LIBRA WORK STYLE

Prefers Consultations ︶ *Sorts Facts* ︶ *Is Diplomatic*

Libra does not fare well in sterile cubicles with hard angles. Libra wants to be surrounded with warm tones, cozy fabrics, and people who partner with him well. He has photos of himself with nearly everyone who has crossed his path. Unlike some of the more overtly ambitious signs, Libra does not get these mementos as a photo op, but as a personal memory. A social animal, Libra gives equal importance to after hours: who he is having dinner with, which social functions to attend.

Libra listens to nearly every opinion on a project before he acts. Early in his decision-making process, Libra will schedule, for example, four appointments in one day regarding how to manage a department.

After the first appointment, Libra feels receptive to the presentation, or at least that was the opinion of the person who presented. Armed with a set of facts and leaning toward what he just heard, Libra is prepared for appointment two. This appointment also goes well, and Libra appears to have responded favorably. In fact, he punctuates the conference with a great deal of "Well, now this is impressive" and "I like the sound of that."

Much to the maddening frustration of the presenters, each feels that an unspoken bargain was made, an agreement was reached; and yet, Libra comes up with another idea altogether. For while Libra may appear like he is mush, easily plied and played, the reality is Libra is a strong person with a fact-driven, fact-sorting, and decisive mind. Once his mind is made up, after taking in all the information, thinking and rethinking his decision process, he becomes very clear. Until then, his methods may appear conflicted to the rest of us.

Lee Iacocca says of his work style that he gathers "all the charts and numbers but in the end you have to bring all your information together, set up a timetable, and act." Iacocca says that he has been described as flamboyant and a shoot-from-the-hip sort of guy. Iacocca disagrees, however, and declares his style is totally unlike that. In fact, Iacocca "acts on intuition only when my hunches are supported by fact."

It is a testament to Libra that he can change his beautiful colors in business. One can imagine him as a seat-of-the-pants CEO, when in reality Libra can be one well-thought-out and tough cookie. Libra can sneak up on you because of this.

THE LIBRA STRENGTHS

Social Skills ♎ *A Deal Maker* ♎ *Strong Emotional IQ*

In a word, grace. Grace is the soft answer to anger. Grace is the search for what is fair, the ability to incorporate compromise and make it sound like a win-win.

While many different kinds of intelligence exist, each astrological sign possesses one or more areas in which they are most likely to exceed. The Libra has a strong emotional IQ and functions best when utilizing his innate ability to get along with others, develop their good character traits, and defuse stress and disharmony.

Individuals who have strong emotional intelligence can handle the ups and downs of life. Libra, the astrological sign of balance, can understand the cycles in life, the failures and triumphs, and handle them with grace and a sense of calm.

In *7 Kinds of Smart: Identifying and Developing Your Multiple Types of Intelligences*, author Armstrong describes Gardner's theory of the different IQs. His discussion of "people smart" closely relates to another of the strengths of the Libra IQ, interpersonal skills.

Libra excels in leadership when it involves teamwork, bringing groups together, and bringing out the best in others. While Aries yells "Fire!" and Taurus counts monies, Libra looks for ways to understanding, routes to deal making, solutions for concerns. Libra is a fixer, a peacemaker, a partner in the making. But, for all his compassion and human interest, Libra has his own agenda and is formidable.

THE LIBRA FAVORITE WORK ENVIRONMENT

Public Service Buildings ⚖ *Personalized Settings*

In a world of videoconferencing, Libra loves a conference that is eye to eye. He can be found at round tables, such as Gandhi attended in London during his release from prison. Such is the magnitude of Libra at work. Know of anyone else who got released from prison to help with peace talks? Libras, such as President Carter, somehow manage to be summoned for peace summits and last-ditch efforts to counsel and conciliate.

Libra prefers intimate surroundings in which to work his considerable charm. His nearly ingratiating ways shine in three-ring circus settings like American politics or working with elected officials. In these arenas, he is a standout.

Kibitzers, lobbyists, advocates, and commissioners rely on Libra to listen to what people are really saying, gather information, and find what has merit. Many elected officials have relied on the Libra gift of facilitating compromise and middle ground in policy-making situations.

Libra can be found at public administration addresses, his benevolent smile greeting you along the way as he informs or recruits you. You can be sure that wherever Libra begins his career, he will eventually want to be in control. He knows he was born with winning ways. And win he will.

Even when Sarah Ferguson had her little slip from grace and all the attending difficulties, she landed on her feet as only lovely Libra can. Don't we all just love her for this?

THE LIBRA EMPLOYEE/COWORKER

Persuasive ⚖ *A Good Listener* ⚖ *Vague*

Who is your new pal at work? Who can't stand it when Fred and Frank quarrel? The Libra. Libra doesn't do much alone and is usually not found off in a corner reading a book on weekends. Libra collects personalities, individuals, and portions of other souls; a solitary state, therefore, is most unlikely.

Libra loves music, the arts, and good company. Talented in artistic endeavors, he often seeks out art fairs and museum openings in his off time. Libra spends time at home weekends or holidays when working on renovating his home, remodeling, or redecorating. Skilled naturally along these lines, he enjoys puttering around.

Libra is the solution to morale problems at work and can keep things running smoothly. Disharmony and conflict make him physically ill. He will not work in situations that eliminate the human factor, that ignore individual rights and feelings. Libra is the "co" in coworker. All else revolves around that.

Eisenhower said, "The best morale exists when you never hear the word mentioned. When you hear a lot of talk about it, it is usually lousy." Libra is astute and has a way of summarizing issues like this.

Faced with failure or a temporary setback, Libra looks for ways to work around the decisions or the powers that be to renegotiate a project or persuade new approaches to eventually regain control.

An example of the Libra negotiating style is former President Jimmy Carter who decided to run for president three years before he formally announced his plan to run. Behind the scenes, he had drawn up a detailed campaign strategy and kept an exhausting campaign schedule. At the time, Carter was nationally unknown for the most part and an outsider to Washington, as well. But his negotiations for the highest office in the land began with his ability to win votes—that old Libra popularity quotient.

Carter parlayed his popularity with the Libra vagueness. His carefully strategized work was not apparent to the general public, only his charm and soft-spoken manner. His campaign was based primarily on his personality.

President Dwight D. Eisenhower, another Libra who parlayed his public approval, used "I like Ike" for his campaign slogan. When dealing with Libra, remember, he has the six-second advantage. It is important to know that critical first impressions usually occur within the first six seconds of meeting someone. Libra wins hands down in the first impressions department. And, frankly, it takes a lot to undo that, especially if he remains inexplicit.

Libra is adept at getting his way and maneuvering to any position, without raising any warning flags. While acting like either choice is OK, or it's six of one and half dozen of the other, he has a preference and a plan. Libra keeps things vague and iffy for a reason.

Libra is good at persuasion. He hones this skill by listening, being sensitive to others, and learning to nurture. Like any good persuader or salesperson, the Libra coworker knows when to make the pitch, what objections to overcome, and how to close the deal. Libra does not stand up to authority, but sits down in face-to-face negotiations.

By the time Libra unveils his agenda, you are ready to make the deal. He does not need excessive self-promotion, divide-and-conquer tactics, or demanding, berating stratagems. Instead, you and he will be sipping mint juleps together when the announcement is made.

THE LIBRA LEARNING STYLE

Logical △ Deliberate △ Structured

The way a Libra learns or the way in which his mind works is considered concrete when viewed in the context of the Gregorc Model of Learning Styles.

Everyone and every sign observe the same sights and sounds, yet each perceives them in different ways. While at some level we all see what we want to see, we still convert information in two distinct fashions. One perceptual quality is a concrete learning style.

When you think or perceive in a concrete way, you tend to check out all the possibilities and check out every angle before you make decisions. Libra is the decision maker of the zodiac. He weighs the evidence, like his symbol the scales, before committing to a solution or judgment. Searching for knowledge, Libra may need excessive information.

For example, Libra likes his information organized, factual, consistent, and dependable. He needs to verbalize about matters up for consideration, to debate and ponder. Libra needs an explanation for everything, requires time to deliberate, and relies on numbers. Go to the department of pie in the sky for plans that are not fully documented or ready for presentation and bypass Libra.

While all of us process information from both a concrete and an abstract viewpoint, we have a preference. This preference is where we are most comfortable in learning and working situations. Libra can understand long-range and reality-based dreams, but he wants a surefire way to implement them.

The second component to learning is how we order our information. Libra prefers structured, logical, measurable methods of organizing information. This preference is called a sequential learning style. This inclines the Libra to learn better when he is given a chance to follow his own pace, utilize his own systems, and conceptualize an idea first before making a decision. This is all part of the Libra work style, so when approaching him, bring the three Ds: data, documents, and details.

THE BEST WAY FOR A LIBRA TO LEARN

Needs Concise Presentations ︎ *Works Well in Partnering*

Libra is in no hurry to be given assignments or tackle projects. Libra, while impressive, is more low-key and less energetic than most of the other signs. He does not react quickly, prefers a slower pace, and prefers to know what is happening or expected to happen on any given day. Libra likes to feel he is in control.

While other signs may be excited by streams of new assignments and lots of challenges, Libra likes projects and tasks that have limits and boundaries. Without boundaries, he never quite comes to that long-anticipated decision.

Libra listens to others who take risks with a sort of giggling awe. Intellectual challenges are enough to satisfy Libra. He likes to be given options to research and figure out what needs to be done. He does not work well with stifling members of management who do not allow for his personal approach to work.

While, more than any other sign, Libra works from both random and abstract perceptions, his need for harmony, team effort, and flexibility is outweighed by his logical, objective framework. Approach his training sessions by making concise statements and present material in a logical sequence. Flying by the seat of your pants will amuse and delight him, but this will not be the best way for Libra to retain information. Offer him a chance to work in teams or partner with another in role-playing sessions.

If you want to work with or for a Libra, remember that he has an abstract/sequential learning style. He is people oriented. He is of the thoughtful air sign element and the cardinal mode astrologically. As a cardinal type, Libra is inclined to be more ambitious than the other signs. He is fully capable of biding his time, knowing that success will come.

THE LIBRA PROFILE

A Diplomat ⎵ *Realizes There Is Strength in Numbers*

Libra can tame the savage beast, get the lions and lambs to lie down together, because his conciliatory, diplomatic gifts are of that elevated caliber.

You will not see Libra beating his chest, pulling his hair out, or displaying any other antics. His manner is calm, soothing, and even in all aspects of his personality. The Libra modus operandi at work is recognizing that there is strength in numbers; and his role is to build his numbers, polls, and ratings one coworker at a time.

When Libra combines in a working relationship with a water sign of Cancer, Scorpio, or Pisces, steam occurs. Steam pushes along the water, and together they can work miracles around bureaucratic red tape.

In the same way, the energies of the fire signs of Aries, Leo, and Sagittarius are compatible and inspiring. The off-the-cuff manner of the Sagittarius holds a certain fascination for the Libra. The all-impulse approach of Aries provides the missing ingredient for the Libra. Libra is captivated by Aries' independence. Libra wishes he could gain this sense of autonomy by osmosis. In that respect, the Aries can assist the Libra in more independent ventures.

When the Libra sun combines with the earth signs of Taurus, Virgo, and Capricorn in working relationships, reactions are interesting. Libra has an innate understanding with Taurus whose love of beauty, harmony, and music is compatible with Libra. Virgo is too impersonal for Libra in long-term assignments. Capricorn's ambitions find a match in Libra's aspirations. Capricorn will speak their desires into the ethers and anywhere else they might be heard. Libra wants to downplay their aspirations.

When Libra combines in a working relationship with one of his fellow air signs, such as Gemini or Aquarius, you can expect great accomplishments. Libra can soothe the ups and downs of the Gemini and keep the Aquarius from taking too many trips to the planetarium during the workday. These thinking signs have a tendency to live in their heads and are great in think tanks together. Brainstorming is a natural by-product of their interaction.

THE LIBRA BOSS

Seeks Opinions ⎍ *Is Ambitious*

Libra cares about you. He is even-tempered. He is adorable, but he will be decisive about your termination if he thinks you are no longer an asset or have slacked off in your commitment to his agenda.

Libra wants a smooth operation, harmonious without ruffled feathers and angry confrontations. He really cannot and will not stand for emotional disruption at work. It affects his blood sugar levels.

While Libra works at what appears to be a slower pace, he is actually fevered with ambition. He instinctively looks for a work partner and will test this out by asking for everyone's opinion on just about everything. Then, when he discovers someone who can augment or complement his natural talents, he makes his choice for assistant, associate, or partner. This choice, of utmost importance in his career, may even be someone outside his work environment, but you can be sure Libra's ideas are not 100 percent his own.

Ever had dinner out with a Libra boss or business owner with clients? He is the warm host, sparing no expense, the setting memorable. Libra talks about sports, vacation spots, and how much he loves his neighbors. The conversation does not turn to business, deals, or clients. If it does, he becomes vague and steers things back to people. His business is not about business, but relationships.

LIBRA SUCCESS STORIES

Ray Kroc of McDonald's started out the 1980 annual report with "Quality is the first word in the McDonald's Motto of QSC&V (Quality, Service, Cleanliness and Value)."

Kroc got nearly misty-eyed over the beauty of his hamburger buns. He recognized the importance of beauty in selling his product. And, he honored basic values in the QSC&V for his customers. Libra must always consider what his work can do for others, whether it is in the simple act of putting together a great looking hamburger, building a beautiful house, or negotiating the return of an ousted president of Haiti.

Eisenhower and Carter showed the importance of the likability of Libra. Carter has gone on to become a capable negotiator and a great humanitarian. It was President Carter who set the framework for the peace between Israel and Egypt. He also signed the second Strategic Arms Limitation Treaty with the USSR. While Carter was a successful businessman, more importantly he was a successful human being. He has nurtured his soul doing what Libra does so well—facilitating peace and working toward human rights.

John Lennon wrote about giving peace a chance, demonstrated for love not war, and left us with poignant memories of his hopes for mankind.

Whether Libra writes, sings, or lectures, words like peace and love spill out of his mouth. Whether at round tables, conference tables, or dinner tables, Libra wants to help us love one another, one person at a time.

Lawyers, lobbyists, arbitrators, all working their Libra enchantments to good ends, find inspiration in the "great-soul" of Mohandas Gandhi. Gandhi was able to unify the Indian National Congress. When disputes broke out, he prayed for pacification and espoused passive resistance. He taught us that words can be mightier than any sword. Gandhi preached Christian, Moslem, and Hindu ethics. Libra doesn't like to leave anyone or anyone's beliefs out.

A surprisingly large percentage of Libras have strong religious training or good old-fashioned Sunday school backgrounds, like Eisenhower's. Lennon grew up with a puritanical Methodist grandmother and remarked that her influence stayed with him, some of which you can hear in his lyrics.

From early Sunday school to prayers at rallies, from treating people well to creating public policy, Libra puts the emphasis on his fellow man; without it, Libra would find no inspiration.

⚖

OTHER FAMOUS LIBRAS

Armand Assante	Heather Locklear
Neve Campbell	Gwyneth Paltrow
Joan Cusack	Luke Perry
Matt Damon	Susan Sarandon
Jenna Elfman	Alicia Silverstone
Jeff Goldblum	Barbara Walters
Evander Holyfield	Kate Winslet
Julio Iglesias	Catherine Zeta-Jones

RESOURCES

Drain, Patricia Noel. 1992. *Hire Me! Secrets of Job Interviewing*. Los Angeles: Price Stern Sloan Publishers.

Goldman, Albert. 1988. *The Lives of John Lennon*. New York: William Morrow.

Iacocca, Lee, and William Novak. 1984. *Iacocca: An Autobiography*. New York: Bantam Books.

Peters, Thomas J., and Robert H. Waterman Jr. 1982. *In Search of Excellence: Lessons from America's Best-Run Companies*. New York: Warner Books.

CHAPTER 8

THE STRATEGIST

SCORPIO ■ OCTOBER 23 TO NOVEMBER 23

HOW TO SPOT A SCORPIO

Powerful ♏ *A Strategist* ♏ *Secretive*

A little black magic defines the steps of Scorpio as he swaggers toward you, making him easy to recognize. This boldness in his walk is his signature at the office and in life. With a throaty voice, he speaks with almost a whisper.

The Scorpio projects an insolent, brash, and often machismo air that may or may not be what he is feeling. When Scorpio enters the room, or stands next to you in the elevator, you sense power.

With the same daring, Scorpio approaches his life and his career. He is the warrior of the workforce, willing his way to his ultimate ambition.

Scorpio examines any and all directions or procedures. His laserlike focus demands more than guidelines. Scorpio wants boundaries, lines drawn in the sands, and time to consider his vantage point. He does not usually misplace things, rather obscures them from scrutiny until he is ready to reveal his work or his investigations.

Through sleepy eyes, Scorpio sees what others miss with the insights of a general. There is nothing halfway or indecisive about

Scorpio. His speech is neither vague nor blunt, but cuttingly to the point. His signature, his ink, which has started or ended many negotiations or wars, is courageous with every flourish and dotted *i*.

One of Scorpio's most notable characteristics is that he is organized and thorough, committed to persevere, to follow orders, and to command. Everything starts in the Scorpio mind, for Scorpio knows that where there is a will there is indeed a way.

Like his ruler, the eagle, Scorpio builds his nest high, adding to his territory year after year. Myths about his abilities persist even when Scorpio appears ordinary.

Secrecy surrounds the mysterious Scorpio, a scandal perhaps, but always something of an ignominy in his reputation. And so a Scorpio at work invokes some awe, some touch of the hair standing up on your neck. Above all, Scorpio is a force, a presence in any organization.

Scorpio often ends up in investigative fields: the private investigator, reporter, security analyst, police person, auditor, estate planner, sculptor, surgeon, or military leader.

Since the beginning of time, Scorpio has used his desire and strength to obtain his goals. Struggling with issues of self-mastery and control, he learns to channel the resources of others rather than becoming the scavenger or the corporate raider. From this, he learns that it is often wiser to make opportunities rather than find them.

WHAT DRIVES THE SCORPIO?

Passion ♏ *Lure of the Hidden*

Scorpio cannot be reasoned with, dominated, or structured unless his sense of discovery, the lure of the hidden, is aroused. Scorpio must be motivated by his passion. Oh, he dreams of financial security beyond the ordinary; he craves security. Still, it is his passion that allows him to amass a fortune. But, only if he wants to. Scorpio does nothing unless he desires to do it.

The slow, methodical methods of the earth signs Taurus, Virgo, and Capricorn are greatly admired by the Scorpio. He and the Capricorn work well together, both going for the win. Yet, they can be enemies when in competition because one has to be the winner and neither can stand to lose. Taurus and Scorpio make money together.

The air signs, Gemini, Libra, and Aquarius, with their lack of total commitment and dedication, leave the Scorpio frustrated. Scorpio, above all, is intense. He has no tolerance for the iffy, the untried, or the lackadaisical, which is what he considers the untested.

Fire signs Aries, Leo, and Sagittarius are said to have their fires extinguished by the water element. Actually, fire and water can create steam to combust the engine of progress. Aries and Scorpio have a natural affinity for one another, each recognizing the combatantlike nature of the other.

Fellow water signs Cancer and Pisces understand the undisclosed, private side of Scorpio. They all experience the flashes of presentiment that are particular to each of them. As Einstein, a Pisces, said, "Imagination is more important than knowledge." Imagination is the strong motivator of the three signs.

THE SCORPIO WORK STYLE

Likes Order ♏︎ *Works Well with Deadlines* ♏︎ *Prefers Challenges*

Scorpio wants an ordered office, his work often laid out in rows or neat stacks so that he can keep his eagle eye on everything. Metal sculptures and modern art surround him, a few battle relics here and there. He prefers a dark office, a bit foreboding. Scorpio is not waiting for visitors. He has his lucky bird-of-paradise in a pot, and most likely he wears a ring of topaz or bloodstone for protection. Scorpio believes in talismans and omens, unaware that his charisma is his very own talisman.

Dark colors, black and burgundy reds in particular, attract Scorpio. Professional golfer Gary Player adopted an all-black wardrobe as a trademark. Scorpio frequently wears all-black clothing with a touch of blood red for contrast.

As you may have surmised, Scorpio loves challenges, for he is a person who never doubts his ability to master a situation. Scorpio prefers a pace that allows him to explore the possibilities. Yet, he wants deadlines, dates of closure, and resolution.

Given new tasks, the Scorpio excels in reinventing the wheel, revitalizing the company, and recreating the image of the entire company. Scorpio is awesome in his abilities when given perimeters for his particular talents. He needs structure, however, as he does have a tendency to be his own worst enemy when left alone for too long.

THE SCORPIO STRENGTHS

Investigative Intelligence ♏ *Imaginative* ♏ *Endures Much*

While many different kinds of intelligence exist, each astrological sign possesses one or more areas in which they are most likely to excel. The Scorpio has a strong constitution and recuperative powers. But while he is able physically, he functions best at an investigative level. Scorpio is able to use the three I's—imagination, intuition, and intelligence—to discover the new and uncover the hidden.

Scorpio has a sixth sense and is not afraid to use it in business. He is sturdy and can endure much. He is not apprehensive about getting to the bottom of anything. Like his symbol, the eagle (called the winged wolf by the Aztecs), Scorpio can see beyond the scope of others. This is the sort of vision that no doubt guided Bill Gates.

Sometimes, making a foresight a reality can isolate Scorpio from others. Such is the price of those with the gift of insight.

THE SCORPIO FAVORITE WORK ENVIRONMENT

Businesses That Investigate ♏︎ *Positions That Deal with Life and Death*

Scorpio works best in limited environments. He does not like to be lost in a crowd or a long corridor of cubicles. Allow him some privacy, some space. Believing in the magic of numbers, he works best in a suite containing the numbers eight or two. As always for Scorpio, believing makes it so.

Look around the office of the Scorpio. Chances are the lighting is soft, not harsh or natural. Scorpio prefers soft music and often silence. He has the ever-present coffee cup and chocolates nearby, a mystery novel hidden in a drawer, and photos of a recent scuba diving adventure.

You may find the portrait of his long-lost love on his desk, as there is surely one in his past. Perhaps this is part of the gossip surrounding him. Do not ask for details.

The Pluto-ruled Scorpio is a law unto himself. He will not be concerned with what you think. He will not care if you agree with him. And finally, he will not particularly care if you like him, although you will certainly be fascinated by him, as he is irresistible.

Scorpio is not afraid to give a straightforward answer. He can say both yes and no with ease. He does not feel compelled to do anything except answer to his own demons.

You may find him near chalk lines, at police stations, the IRS, or FBI. Scorpio may also be found investigating at a major stock firm, in the military, or at the local hospital. Whatever his arena, it is a serious one.

THE SCORPIO EMPLOYEE/COWORKER

Intense ♏ *A Survivor* ♏ *Tries to Keep His Word*

Scorpio is, for all his intensity, a cool person and exciting to be around. He is intelligent and has a wonderful if somewhat caustic wit. He gravitates toward excitement and intrigue in and out of work. Scorpio is not, however, afraid to spend time alone, for he always has a pet project in progress.

Jonas Salk, the epidemiologist whose passion occupied most of his life, exemplifies Scorpio. Salk spent many hours in his research laboratory in Pittsburgh, discovering a vaccine for polio. Like Salk, your Scorpio coworker is toiling at some discovery or another as you read this.

A Scorpio experiencing a morale problem will involve himself in all the plots and subplots. Scorpio is a black-and-white employee. He believes in them and us, good and bad, superior and inferior. Whatever thwarts or slows his rise in the firm will be viewed as bad, and he is ready to rise like the warrior he is. His tension electrifies the air. There may be outbursts, sullen days, and the stare. Nothing can prepare you for THE STARE. The eyes of the eagle, sharp and penetrating, go to the soul. His eyes reveal his inner turmoil.

Still, it is this intensity, this touch of the ruthless, that makes him one of the natural survivors of the zodiac. It is important to remember that the real threat to Scorpio is not the animosity sometimes found in tense situations, but the Scorpio himself. It is Scorpio who is his own unstoppable enemy when all is said and done. This is why it is vital for the Scorpio to befriend himself, to not get lost in corporate battle. Scorpio should remember to park his grudge in the company lot, in his "Reserved for the CEO" space.

Scorpio can fight for or against you in supervision he deems unfair. All he needs is to believe in you or your visions. He can, therefore, be a staunch ally.

Scorpio commands respect. He is not afraid to stand up for his beliefs or ask for corrective action for an injustice or oversight. He will honor commitments. He says what he means and means what he says.

In *The Magic of Getting What You Want: The Blueprint for Personal Fulfillment,* the author explains that keeping promises will bring big rewards in business. He gives three rules to follow:

1. Keep appointments and keep them on time.
2. Keep the little promises as well as the big ones.
3. Keep a confidence confidential.

Scorpio has the innate ability to keep his word. His word is important to him. It is a rare Scorpio who will not stand up to his commitments.

Ultimately, the Scorpio is an excellent team builder. He can transform, persuade, and lead.

THE SCORPIO LEARNING STYLE

Is Imaginative ℥ *Prefers Instructions in Writing* ℥ *Asks Questions*

The way a Scorpio learns, or the way in which his mind works, is considered abstract when viewed in the context of the Gregorc Model of Learning Styles.

Everyone and every sign observe the same sights and sounds, yet each perceives them in different ways. While at some level we all see what we want to see, we still convert information in two distinct fashions.

Everyone uses both concrete and abstract reasoning, but the Scorpio learns best when he can use his intelligence and his imagination. Scorpio can see things as they can be, not necessarily as they appear to be or as everyone else sees them. This perceptual preference or quality is called abstract intelligence.

When you think or perceive in an abstract way, you have the ability to visualize. Scorpio has searing insights. He seems to have been born with a sixth sense as well because he often taps into insights that others miss. Scorpio can see that many times there is more to a situation than meets the eye.

Scorpio can see what lies ahead, and he uses that certain uncanny wisdom that is part of his nature to see what is beyond the physical here and now.

The second component to learning is how we order our information. The Scorpio prefers information presented in a step-by-step, organized, clear manner. This preference is called a sequential learning style.

Scorpio likes to get his information in writing. He wants you to sign on the dotted line. Scorpio will probe and ask lots of questions. He wants to know where you got your facts and how he can find out more information than just the basics. When you see Scorpio surfing the Internet, he may very well be researching something on-line.

Scorpio wants to know:

- "Where did this report originate?"
- "What was the basis for these directives?"
- "When do you expect me to finalize this project?"

THE SCORPIO BOSS

Is Intense ♏ *Likes Logical Employees* ♏ *Does Not Tip His Hand*

Scorpio assumes that all employees possess some natural curiosity and logical thought. He really doesn't understand anyone who does not. Beyond that, he hopes you have some creativity. If he believes in you, the sky is the limit for you working for him. He will push you along on his path to prosperity.

So what is the Plutonian man like? Really? He is a winner. Scorpio is intent on his goals, quiet in his pursuit. He is the calm before the storm, not the storm itself. Don't tie yourself up in knots worrying that he is explosive. He has such self-control that he seldom tips his hand with a tirade.

Sarcasm is Scorpio's trademark. A friend of mine, a newspaper editor, heard one sarcastic remark too many from her Scorpio boss toward one of her coworkers. She had reached the point where she could no longer hold her tongue; she would not tolerate working for a man who, in her mind, could be so cruel to her associates. Job be damned, she was going to tell him off.

This normally cool, aloof Capricorn (as it turned out) employee marched right up to his enormous glass office and told him what she thought of his behavior. He was stern as always, and she was thinking of where she should send her resume. He stared at her in disbelief, then spoke, "I am sorry if I offended you."

She walked out, admittedly wobbly near the knees. He went back to work. The Scorpio boss never bothered to apologize to the coworker, but the incident was over.

The Scorpio boss was promoted to a top-ten-market newspaper, and, out of his entire staff, he made one job offer. It was to the Capricorn, who he said he admired for her courage. A warrior always holds some grudging respect for another of spirit.

Scorpio, like the rest of us, will make misjudgments on his path to success. Usually, these errors are about control issues. He has trouble delegating and doesn't know when to let go.

When Scorpio faces opposition at work, he often takes it personally and holds a grudge. Scorpio isn't above a few dirty tricks. We usually know he is trying to avenge himself but just can't quite prove it. Scorpio is never overt.

It is important to note, however, that there are three kinds of Scorpio: the scorpion who is a downright scoundrel (there are few of these around, however), the eagle who is the typical Scorpio, and the dove who is the most evolved of the three types or the Billy Graham of Scorpios.

SCORPIO SUCCESS STORIES

Bill Gates is an excellent example of the Scorpio temperament, representing the passionate, stupendous, all-consuming white-hot fire in the soul that determines a person's course. Gates had the passion of the soaring eagle; with his amazing power of will, he took his vision of a "computer on every desk and in every room," and made it a reality.

One component of Gates's immense success has been his marketing strategy. His ideas for marketing were fueled in part by his ability to make leaps from single sets of information to the larger picture.

The passion of dovelike orator Billy Graham fueled his inner flame to crusade for his beliefs. The famous evangelist had the forceful, charismatic persona that wins souls. He brought awareness of man's need to connect to something bigger than himself, beyond himself to light. The dove understands the stirring of another's heart.

Elizabeth Cady Stanton led the woman's suffrage movement along with Susan B. Anthony, working on women's issues and actively fighting against slavery. The warrior, Stanton introduced support of a divorce bill. The Scorpio religious bent was evident when Stanton wrote *The Woman's Bible.*

Stanton described herself as a radical. In her farewell speech, she declared, "Organized religion is at the roots of repression of women." Believing this in her heart, she organized unions, conventions, and demonstrations.

Stanton summed up Scorpio in seven words when she wrote, "Courageous, I put my soul into everything." Has there ever been a Scorpio who did not?

♏

OTHER FAMOUS SCORPIOS

Troy Aikman   Goldie Hawn
Hillary Clinton   Robert Kennedy
Dennis Franz   Natalie Merchant
Whoopi Goldberg   Demi Moore
Deidre Hall   Jane Pauley
Edmond Halley   Julia Roberts
Ethan Hawke

RESOURCES

Bachar, Jacqueline. In a lecture based on her upcoming book, *Elizabeth Cady Stanton: America's Grand Old Woman.*

Schwartz, David J. 1984. *The Magic of Getting What You Want: The Blueprint for Personal Fulfillment.* New York: Berkley Books.

CHAPTER 9

THE POLITICIAN

SAGITTARIUS ▪ NOVEMBER 23 TO DECEMBER 22

HOW TO SPOT A SAGITTARIUS

Inspiring ⚹ Verbal ⚹ Restless

Sagittarius doesn't just dash about; he fairly runs. A little awkward, usually long and gangly, he is the colt or the racehorse of the zodiac. And, occasionally, he is a thoroughbred like the late John Kennedy Jr.

Usually a spirit of excitement surrounds Sagittarius. He was born to lead and inspire. Oh, sure, he can get down in the dumps like anyone else, but he can jump the fence and move on if things get too gloomy.

Tina Turner took only her name and her aspirations when she decided to find a better life. After her ordeal, a troubled, abusive marriage, she told her story, a story of inspiration and self-reliance that gives us all courage in difficult times. Sagittarius is never afraid to tell his story. And in doing so, he inspires us.

Sagittarius probably lost the personnel guidelines a few times before he attempted to read them. Then he wiggled, squirmed, got up to stretch his long legs, and ultimately forgot part of what he read. It won't matter. Whatever Sagittarius remembers will be just the right thing. For Sagittarius is lucky, you see. Never forget that when you watch his work style. A good portion of his success will be based on plain old good fortune.

One of Sagittarius's most notable characteristics is that he is physical—the tennis champ, the baseball Hall of Famer, the left-handed pitcher, the hockey player, the swimmer; and just to prove he is lucky, his horses win four Kentucky Derbys.

A dual sign, Sagittarius can do many things well. He is also the philosopher and politician. He is the mayor, the abolitionist, the founder of the Chinese army, the king of Serbs, the chancellor of West Germany, the Russian anarchist, the nationalist revolutionary leader, the president, the founder of a church. Right wing and left wing, liberal and conservative, Sagittarius is always leading something. And, he is particularly fascinated with politics.

Sagittarius is quick, restless, and more often than not, eccentric. He speaks without censure, and his enthusiasm spills from his mouth in a shower of words. He is fired up and ready for action. Sagittarius is friendly as a pup, eager and jumpy.

Since the beginning of time, Sagittarius has been involved in compelling pursuits that satisfy the physical, mental, and spiritual. The last of the fire signs, he brings the talent of the Aries and Leo to full bloom. The Sagittarian strives to develop his higher mind through increased studies, reverence for the law, and the meaning of religion. Sagittarius searches for wisdom. He dreams of instructing, teaching, and publishing, and these dreams come true usually without much forethought.

Sagittarius is the minister, foreign correspondent, ambassador, cowboy or cowgirl, translator, travel agent, publisher, animal caretaker, aviator, and Jack or Jill of all trades.

WHAT DRIVES THE SAGITTARIUS?

Dreams and Aspirations ↗ *Impulses*

Aspirations drive the Sagittarius; like his symbol of the archer, he aims for the stars. While he is restless, energetic, and physical, he takes his desires beyond the physical and into the stratosphere of the mind and all its capabilities.

Sagittarius is never cautious or withholding about his dreams. He tells of them in brilliant oratory and writes about them in fiery publications. He volunteers for multiple causes. He is active in his visions of making the world a better place. However, it should be noted that not all Sagittarians agree on just what is "a better place."

The cautious, slower-paced earth signs of Taurus, Virgo, and Capricorn work surprisingly well with Sagittarius. The earth signs can often pick up the pieces of the Sagittarian's scattered work and energies and pull together a project for him.

The air signs of Gemini, Libra, and Aquarius make Sagittarius nervous with all that pondering, resulting in his tendency to finish their sentences. While they get along well, the fire energies of Sagittarius tend to make giant leaps in logic that leave the mental air signs in the soot. Still, Sagittarius can complete much of Gemini's work in the publishing arena or overseas ventures.

The fellow fire signs of Aries and Leo seem to turn to Sagittarius for the lucky break that they often miss in their own lives. Working together, fast as lightning, they blaze trails. And sometimes along the way Sagittarius, like Nero, burns Rome. Sagittarius needs someone, somewhere to check and countercheck his impulses, wonderful as they might be.

Water signs Cancer, Scorpio, and Pisces seem to repress the Sagittarian's energies. Sagittarius feels hampered by them, referring to them as wet blankets. Yet Pisces' work is often initiated by Sagittarius, just as Einstein's work was enlightened by Spinoza's view of God.

THE SAGITTARIUS WORK STYLE

Responsive to Freedom of Expression ↗ *Playful*

Sagittarius wants to play. He wants to brainstorm and feel he is given the freedom to work in his own way. He likes to stop and get coffee. He likes to walk that cup around from office to office, say hello, and check things out like a nice, nosey neighbor.

Sagittarius needs schedules because free time to him can be taken literally. But, when his environment offers order and allowances for freedom, he has tremendous potential.

A flood of assignments or many interruptions won't bother Sagittarius. In fact, he rather enjoys them. He interprets directions as a starting point for a multitude of imaginative ideas and pursuits, so he doesn't mind them either. However, as he works from chaos, he has an odd way of getting his work done.

THE SAGITTARIUS STRENGTHS

Bodily Kinesthetic ↗ *Highly Energetic* ↗ *Doesn't Mind Interruptions*

While many different kinds of intelligence exist, each astrological sign possesses one or more areas in which they are most likely to excel. The Sagittarius excels at sports and the physical, and functions well there, but he is multifaceted and is more aptly described by bodily kinesthetic intelligence.

Sagittarius, like the jack-of-all-trades that he is, can use his intelligence to demonstrate with bodily movements. People who use their hands are examples of bodily kinesthetic intelligence, and so the Sagittarius is a good mechanic, carpenter, or athlete. Beyond that he can use his power of speech to bring ordinary lectures to life. Sagittarius influences with words as do motivational speakers, actors, orators, and politicians.

The bodily kinesthetic form of intelligence is often associated with unusually high levels of energy. Sagittarius can accomplish multiple tasks at the same time. He can talk on the phone and continue to write his novel. Sagittarius can hear and hold two conversations at once.

Instead of trying to get Sagittarius to slow down or sit still, it is wise to allow him to take breaks, get up, and move around.

THE SAGITTARIUS FAVORITE WORK ENVIRONMENT

Foreign Countries ♐ Outdoors ♐ Cluttered Surroundings

Sagittarius likes to work in the outdoors—engaging in crusades, marching to campaign music, rallying people with megaphones, debating in teams, leading demonstrations.

Often found in sports, Sagittarius, with his flair for words, is the rules interpreter, the referee, the sportscaster, the sportswriter.

Sagittarius likes offices overseas and often excels when working outside his country of origin. Sagittarius likes to conduct business on yachts, golf courses, and ski lifts. He is motivated, indeed enthralled, by new dialects, customs, and procedures.

A Sagittarian will sit on his desk, stack files in his chair, leave cabinets ajar, and work in disarray. He likes it this way. Any attempt to clean it up for him will just distract him. To Sagittarius, clutter is order. Pictures do not need to be hung on the wall to be aesthetically pleasing for him. He may never quite unpack or fully move in either.

If there is any opportunity to bring an animal to work, he will.

Let Sagittarius run to the boarding gate, papers falling and trailing behind him. Some stranger will pick them up for him, run to the gate, and assist him with his journey. Oh, yes, and the perfect stranger will pass Sagittarius his business card. They will strike up a conversation, become acquaintances. Then, as you probably guessed, this unknown individual who came to the aid of the addled Sagittarius will become a valuable business contact.

Sagittarius proves that he can accomplish more by accident than most other signs do on purpose because Sagittarius has the luck of the Irish.

THE SAGITTARIUS EMPLOYEE/COWORKER

Outspoken ↗ *A Maverick* ↗ *Engaging*

Sagittarius loves to have fun. He is witty and full of tales of adventures all over the globe. Good with awkward physical comedy, he likes to flail his arms and legs around for effect when telling his stories.

Sagittarius goes home when there is nowhere else to go. His weekends are spent outdoors in some physical activity. He considers rest a waste of time. Sagittarius does, however, like to read, and he has well-stocked shelves on travel, biography, and adventure books.

Some Sagittarians are discovering Kyudo, which is an excellent way to relieve stress. This Japanese martial art combines archery, balance, and meditation. Meditation like this helps the Sagittarian to vent some energies like impatience and not to chomp at the bit over minor delays in his career path.

When Sagittarius faces a morale problem at work, he is rather shocked. He had no idea there was one. For he is a happy-go-lucky, back-slapping, hail-and-farewell type who doesn't want to think about the negative.

A Sagittarius solution to a morale dilemma is to cheer up everyone with a get-together and some wine. With optimism that all will work out, he doesn't visit problems of any sort for long. In fact, he usually denies them or changes the subject when too many complaints are made.

Sagittarius's enthusiasm inspires and leads his coworkers. In *High-Velocity Culture Change: A Handbook for Managers*, the author speaks about the Sagittarius type of employee. "You want pistols, hot-blooded people bent on making their mark. Not mild mannered, conforming types who will succumb to the awesome power of the existing culture." Sagittarius is always a pistol.

This epitomizes the Sagittarius type of employee. If he could sign his name under the above statement for his job description, the Sagittarius would be signing this instant.

The Sagittarius employee can reshape corporate culture, and management is beginning to recognize this quality. Sagittarius will be a maverick in much the same way December-born Walt Disney was.

Sagittarius was born to inspire. Dale Carnegie, the famous motivational speaker, said, "Most of the important things in the world have been accomplished by people who have kept on trying when there seemed to be no hope at all." Sagittarius, like a bouncing rubber ball, always bounces back from troubles and disappointments. He is the eternal optimist.

The twenty-first-century workforce is about creativity and natural curiosity and the ability to go global. Sagittarius is a perfect fit for this.

Sagittarius is blunt. Very blunt. Although he never intends to, sometimes he hurts your feelings with his outspoken manner.

He rarely loses his temper, excels at working with people, but is hopelessly honest and goofy enough to not understand little white lies. He seems incapable of saying, "I prefer the way you presented the first report," rather than "Yikes, what were you thinking? That presentation was awful."

And, I swear it is true, in spite of his eccentricities, he will charm you, and you will forgive him. Further, you will end up helping him become a success.

THE SAGITTARIUS LEARNING STYLE

Is Aroused by His Curiosity ↗ *Acts on Instinct* ↗ *Uses His Five Senses*

The way a Sagittarius learns, or the way in which his mind works, is dominated by a concrete style when viewed in the context of the Gregorc Model of Learning Styles.

Everyone and every sign observes the same sights and sounds, yet each perceives them in different ways. While at some level we all see what we want to see, we still convert information in two distinct fashions. One perceptual quality is a concrete learning style.

When you think or perceive in a concrete way, you need to register the world around you via the five senses: touch, sight, smell, taste, and hearing. Sagittarian's curiosity, sense of adventure, and spontaneous thinking are all part of the concrete pattern of learning.

For example, Sagittarius is not hesitant to act on impulse, to look for inventive new ways of doing things. He can jump from one idea or topic to another, excels at brainstorming. This is how the concrete thinker prefers to order his information.

If you have a project or business idea to present to Sagittarius, don't be afraid to blurt it out. The worst that can happen is that he will laugh at you with all good nature. You don't have to repeat things for the Sagittarian. In fact, he may finish your sentences for you as he interrupts. His interruptions can be understood as enthusiasms and a nod of approval.

The second component to learning is how we order our information. The Sagittarian prefers loose, unstructured, and fast methods of establishing systems and techniques. This preference involves a random learning style and means that the Sagittarian learns better when given a chance to be the nonconformist, the adventurer, and ultimately the creative person that he is.

Perhaps John Kennedy Jr. instinctively named one of his first companies Random Ventures because he acknowledged his learning style or perceptual preference. He was no by-the-book, step-by-step sort of businessman.

Sagittarius works best from impulse and experimentation, and he may not do the same thing twice, or do something the way it has always been done. Whatever your working relationship with Sagittarius, remember these needs are part of his work style.

While not the best team player, Sagittarius is an excellent coach, a great mentor.

THE BEST WAY FOR A SAGITTARIUS TO LEARN

He Works with Others ↗ *He Has a Hands-On Situation*
Projects Have Deadlines

Sagittarius prefers to jump right in and deal with problems as they arise. Sagittarius likes to be given assignments that allow for creativity. He likes to put his own spin on things. He thrives in a work environment that encourages him to express himself.

Preferring frequent changes in the office, his environment, and his assignments, Sagittarius is quick. He manages to rise to challenges no matter how bumbling he may appear. He wants and needs to be given a deadline. He prefers boundaries on time, otherwise he finds distractions and digresses.

Sagittarius does well in interviewing people, drawing pictures to pass on information, and in job shadowing situations. Extroverted, he likes to work with others. A hands-on situation helps reinforce his learning style.

Change comes naturally to the Sagittarian nature. Because of this, he does well in occupations that require transfers, mergers, and new management from time to time. He genuinely likes other people, is accepting of differences, and allows for individuality in others.

If Sagittarius becomes bored, he can get gloomy. Give him some task and people to juggle, and he will snap right out of it.

THE SAGITTARIUS PROFILE

Extroverted ↗ *Outspoken*

The Sagittarius profile includes his desire to educate and instruct in his work environment and eventually to write about it. He ultimately publishes a thesis, newsletter, manifesto, or novel. Or he may help others publish, for ink is in his blood.

Sagittarius, the last of the three fire signs, helps the other two get the story out, patent the idea, and pull projects out of obscurity after long delays.

Predominately extroverted according to the characteristics of vocational typology, Sagittarius lives the sort of Madison Avenue slogans he inspires. He is about the moment, another idea, and wants to see the possibilities in all things.

Sagittarius excels when speaking for the masses, regardless of the circumstances. He leads, talks, and writes for the common people. Consider this: whether we agree with the politics of the Sagittarian or not, he usually espouses something. Sagittarian-born have been the founder of the John Birch Society, the cofounder of Communism, and the Marxist leader; he is the political agitator, the revolutionary, often the publisher, and invariably the outspoken one.

Forgetful of time, Sagittarius is not one to be concerned about that vexing old appointment book. He may write an appointment down, but he is unlikely to remember to check his calendar.

Just for the fun of it, Sagittarius will try to build a prototype he has not put to paper. Or, just to amuse himself, he will dabble with cartoons and end up a cartoonist—probably accomplished when his rendering fell out of his portfolio at the airport.

Sagittarius possesses a basic kindness that is notable. John Kennedy Jr., for example, took the time to follow a stranger and return a five-dollar bill the stranger had lost. The concern for others is always memorable with Sagittarius.

THE SAGITTARIUS BOSS

Free-Spirited ↗ Tireless ↗ Hasty

Take your vitamins. Sagittarius does not understand low energy levels. Staying out late, partying until the doors slam closed on all activities, is no excuse. Many a Sagittarius has showered and gone to work after such adventures.

Sagittarius doesn't care too much about your personal work style as long as you produce and do not impede his. He likes to see the brighter side of things, as he is the eternal optimist, so don't snivel around him.

Sagittarius, like every other sign, fails in various projects along the way to his ultimate success. But, like other fire signs, individuals with a few failures can learn from their mistakes and make the final giant leap to tremendous success. Don't underestimate Sagittarius because he is different and more than a little hasty.

Sagittarius is hard to pin down. If you need a boss who is your best friend, closest confidant, or right there to help you along, better find another department. Sagittarius is too free-spirited to be that available for anyone. Besides, the Sagittarius aims too high for such mundane matters.

SAGITTARIUS SUCCESS STORIES

Kim Basinger, noted for her eccentricities and love of travel, speaks volumes about the Sagittarius at a work-related social event. In 1990 Basinger, a presenter at the Academy Awards, announced to the audience, "You idiots should have given the Oscar to Spike Lee. Shame on you."

Basinger, a self-proclaimed gypsy at heart, says that if she could, she would "take off in a minute and go live in France for a year. I'd love to live in Africa."

Curtis Hanson, the director of Basinger's Academy Award– winning role in *L.A. Confidential*, says, "Kim is candid: that's the good news and that's the bad news. I don't think she is good at being politic." Good or not, a Sagittarius will always be a political animal of sorts.

John Kennedy Jr., with his dog Friday, skating down the streets of New York on his way to his magazine, *George*, was another example of the tall, lean, athletic, and political Sagittarius.

The magazine was dedicated to the post-partisan mission of its founder. It was over-the-top, offering a refreshing political slant that tried to tell the truth on both sides of party lines. And by all accounts, Kennedy was a roll-up-your-sleeves, hands-on type of publisher. He started in law (no doubt because of a love of debate), but like countless other Sagittarians before him, discovered that publishing intrigued him more.

OTHER FAMOUS SAGITTARIANS

Jeff Bridges	Gena Lee Nolin
Jane Fonda	Nostradamus
Daryl Hannah	Brad Pitt
Teri Hatcher	Keith Richards
Emmett Kelly	Charles Schulz
Jim Morrison	Woodrow Wilson
Nero	

RESOURCES

Bennetts, Leslie. 2000. "The Private Torment of Hollywood's Golden Bombshell," *Vanity Fair* (May).

Pritchett, Price, and Ron Pound. 1994. *High-Velocity Culture Change: A Handbook for Managers*. Dallas, TX: Pritchett and Associates.

CHAPTER 10

THE ADMINISTRATOR

CAPRICORN ■ DECEMBER 22 TO
JANUARY 20

HOW TO SPOT A CAPRICORN

Deliberate ♑ Persistent ♑ Driven

There is something in the take-charge, proper walk of the Capricorn that stands out, just as the slight lisp or slur of his voice. The Capricorn voice is calming, soothing, however, in spite of the unusual quality. His mannerisms are deliberate, and so is his rise to the top.

Capricorn is always the adult child. Capricorn was the teenage rebel in pink and black like Elvis who'd been carrying on with his guitar since he was eleven. Denzel Washington was the first-grade class clown, the actor in bloom. Jeff Bezos of Amazon.com fame dismantled his crib with a screwdriver at the age of three. Tiger Woods played golf at five.

Visible in the young Capricorn are the signs and omens for success and the upward path that he will follow. Capricorn usually has little fun in childhood; he's working already.

The goat was born to scale the top of the mountain. In this same way, the Capricorn-born will surmount all obstacles to achieve his goal. Look to the leaders of any field and you will find a Capricorn.

While Capricorn is unique and his talents vary, his determination to be number one is always his trademark. Oh, yes, he wants to make money, too. Lots of money.

Capricorn is different. He does not have many role models as a result. Capricorn does not feel that imitation is the sincerest form of flattery. He does not do well with mentoring as a result. Early on he is one of a kind; he doesn't want to be like anybody else.

Capricorn is the self-made man or woman. Capricorn is the king of rock, Elvis Presley; the self-proclaimed king of all media, Howard Stern; "I am the greatest" Muhammad Ali; or the queen of country, Dolly Parton. Now, throw in a president or two and you have the power and fortitude of the Capricorn.

Did you know that Elvis started out with a two-dollar guitar? Parton packed up all her clothes in a paper sack and got on a bus to leave the holler and pursue success. Aristotle Onassis, who became one of the richest men of the twentieth century, started his empire with only sixty dollars in his pocket, and of course, the incredible Capricorn ambition.

I know some of you are still stunned at reading that Howard Stern is a Capricorn. We all know and love some conventional, slightly prissy Capricorns and surely, you think, Stern is of another sign. But, the fact is, he is a successful businessman who has risen to the top of his profession. And, he is a man of humble beginnings.

Capricorn often steals the thunder from the royal Leo who likes to lord over everything. It is because of this that Capricorn can be confusing. The Capricorn, however, is the sign of the often disadvantaged individual who gets few lucky breaks. His beginnings are limited as a rule.

Capricorn did not get to the top of the mountain by falling up or off the darn thing. Capricorn got there by persistence and mind-boggling hard work.

So when you see a Capricorn walking toward you, acknowledge his oddity in dress or manner and recognize, too, that this difference may be the thing that makes him the success he will become. After all, where was Elvis without the wiggle, or Ali without the floating-butterfly-and-stinging-bee boxing style?

WHAT DRIVES THE CAPRICORN?

Ambition ℣ Need to Succeed

Capricorn will follow directions, take orders, and keep his day job. But, do not interpret this as acquiescence or acceptance. He has other plans. Acutely aware of time, Capricorn knows he is the late bloomer and is sure that time is on his side. So he will take direction and tutelage, and tow the mark until he arrives. Once he knows what to do or how to do it, he becomes confident in his career, telling others, "It's my job. Just go away and let me do it."

Capricorn often ends up in commerce, public arenas, or public service. Since the beginning of time, Capricorn has been reaching the heights of any given profession, climbing that corporate ladder. He is often found in a government position or working as a principal, statesman, or legal guardian. He is not afraid of heavy burdens or workloads. Like Virgo, Capricorn is the worker of the zodiac.

Ambitious, Capricorn continues on his path of career success in spite of ill health, poverty, or other hardships. Not one for hiding his light, the Capricorn finds his validation in being recognized for his work. Couple these traits with his relentless efforts at attainment, and this sense of responsibility and concern over tradition sets the tone for his leadership style. It is by example as well as ability.

Talk-the-talk, forget-to-walk ideas of the air signs of Gemini, Libra, and Aquarius leave Capricorn feeling like he has wasted time. Of course, Capricorn has not, but he watches the clock and misses the point. This is because Capricorn always wants something to show for his efforts. Exciting nonlinear thinking is often lost on him.

Fire signs Aries, Leo, and Sagittarius do well with Capricorn. They add the zing, the pizzazz, and the touch of good fortune that so often eludes the Capricorn early in life. The fire signs overpower Capricorn's somber quality, get him to lighten up, and remind him that life is not all about work.

It is important to note that the energies of fire and earth are considered favorable astrologically. It is thought that this combination is powerful and that they are the steamrollers of the zodiac.

Water signs Cancer, Scorpio, and Pisces work well with Capricorn. Capricorn makes money off the entrepreneurial Cancer, is impassioned by the Scorpio, and is inspired by the Pisces.

Earth signs like himself, Taurus and Virgo, share many work traits. They all are sturdy, hardworking, traditional sun signs and place a lot of importance on follow-through.

Capricorns seem to respect each other's work. Elvis Presley admired the writer Kahlil Gibran's work. Kevin Costner and Tiger Woods are associates.

THE CAPRICORN WORK STYLE

Time Oriented ꒒ *Punctual* ꒒ *Inconsistent*

Edgar Cayce, the sleeping prophet and twentieth-century clairvoyant described the Capricorn as capricious. This quirk in the Capricorn nature is often missed. But, Capricorn does have a capricious, inconsistent side that, frankly, saves him from being tedious.

♑

The Administrator—Capricorn

A certain way about the Capricorn makes him endearing, such as the way he reveres age, respects his elders, or waltzes Mom around after dinner. He has manners beyond the "thank you" of Elvis and another time. He will cut food for the disabled, remember you love violets, and flash white teeth while smiling at your jokes.

Capricorn can take unconventional paths to his success. He can live on the edge. He can be gaudy or tasteful, understated or over the top, humble or boastful. For this reason, Capricorn is outrageous and success seeking.

Therefore, Capricorn can work in order or in disarray. He works in solitude for days and, then again, calls his mom five times a day. His inconsistent streak is his consistency.

A Capricorn office is sure to have a few rocks from a recent hiking trip and a lovely grandfather clock, perhaps a miniature. Of course, "you know who's" picture will be there among books on every subject. The colors tend toward various tones of brown. If there are drapes, he will usually keep them drawn.

Capricorn likes work heaped on his desk. He likes the in-basket bigger than the out-basket. It adds to his sense of job security. He does not fear diverse duties but constriction and limitations in work.

A stickler for time, he wants a certain amount of freedom in setting his goals. Capricorn will not misuse time, for he reveres it. You can count on him to make deadlines.

It was fellow Capricorn Benjamin Franklin who made the famous statement, "Time is money," and in his book *The Way to Wealth* said, "Do not squander time for it is the stuff that life is made of." When Capricorn peers up at you over his glasses, be ready for your presentation.

Knowing his issues with hours and minutes, do not be late for any appointments with Capricorn.

149

THE CAPRICORN STRENGTHS

Linguistic Intelligence ♑ *A Sense of Timing* ♑ *Determination*

While many different kinds of intelligence exist, each astrological sign possesses one or more areas in which he is likely to excel. The Capricorn has a nearly overwhelming ambitious streak, and this coupled with his organizational strengths helps him excel. But, his intelligence is strongly linguistic, and this in combination with his other attributes makes it possible for him to surpass many.

Capricorn is often a speaker, teacher, writer, or debater. He loves to read and write. He has the gift of words and often studies them. Teach him a new one and watch him delight using it, repeating it with glee.

It is the ability to plan, implement, observe each opportunity and, in fact, make opportunities for himself that makes Capricorn so adept at scaling the heights of any mountain. He often sees the stumbling blocks as little more than stepping-stones.

His linguistic intelligence helps others perceive Capricorn as intelligent or smart and gives him a head start in business transactions. His ability to organize is especially useful when business is being acquired, merged, downsized, or restructured in any way.

Capricorn excels in taking charge, understanding how he can be part of the organization or change, and protecting himself and his career. Capricorn will look for the benefit that change brings. People who make it to the top, the great managers and supervisors, often possess these combinations of characteristics.

Capricorn, the sign of business, is a natural for having his own business. In the meantime, he is invaluable as an employee. Employers find the best employees act as if they own the business in terms of performance. As organizations reshape themselves for the twenty-first century and the entrepreneurial spirits of today, they realize there is a certain benefit to this change. In *New Work Habits for a Radically Changing World,* author Price Pritchett states that employees who take responsibility for themselves and their work are the keys to ultimate success.

Always responsible from a young age, the Capricorn looks for ways to cut costs, improve production, and provide better service to valued customers. Capricorn shines in these areas, as he is independent and takes charge—often a one-person show.

Capricorn is usually troubled with ill health as a child. But, he becomes stronger as he matures and remains healthy into old age. He is conservative in all things and moderate as a rule, but when Capricorn takes that curve, goes 'round that bend, he can do some detrimental things to his constitution.

Once Capricorn starts stepping out of the obedient child role, he becomes outrageous. All these phases are part of his inconsistency. All his inconsistencies are part of his evolvement and eventual success.

Elvis was a well-mannered, almost shy young man when he started wiggling his hips. This hip action was unthinkable in the '50s, yet it became his trademark.

Rush Limbaugh, Howard Stern, and Dr. Laura Schlessinger are all outrageous in their own way—each one of them playing with words, and with us. Because you see, Stern found fame shocking us. Schlessinger, a self-appointed moral watchdog, found her niche and opportunity in scolding us.

Capricorn is born with a special sense of time. He waits for that opportune moment. He knows when he is ready to record that first song, enter that first tournament, start up his own dot.com business. He has been waiting for that moment all his life.

Benjamin Franklin, who started writing at seven, carried the Capricorn themes of his love for words and reverence for time when he made postal reforms that placed emphasis on speed.

THE CAPRICORN FAVORITE
WORK ENVIRONMENT

Academic, Legislative, and Corporate Arenas
Challenging Environments

Capricorn loves top floors, penthouses, boardrooms, and club-houses. Thus, he does well in state legislature, school administration, and any place where he can be part of the architecture of leadership and management.

Wherever he is, he is in preparation for his ultimate rise, waiting for that propitious moment, day, or opportunity.

Unlike many other signs, Capricorn enjoys the office, the desk, and the activity of high-pressure environments. He may look like the intellectual professor, with the tweeds, the wire glasses, and the articulate speech whose only concern is the discussion at hand, but he is, in actuality, plotting higher ground, his next move, and a prestigious appointment here or there.

He likes arenas that offer challenges, debates, or a few obstacles along the way. But the American dream calls to him. He will be unstoppable in these environments.

THE CAPRICORN EMPLOYEE/COWORKER

True to Himself ♑ *Driven* ♑ *Given to Periods of Solitude*

You've probably read just enough to think that Capricorn will not be your favorite coworker with all his nothing-will-stop-me, nothing-will-top-me traits. But, he possesses a dry wit and self-deprecating humor and is often one of the silliest-as-a-billy-goat persons you will ever meet. And, when he desires, he can weave his homespun charm around you, and you fall victim to every wink, giggle, and cooing word.

Capricorn is loyal, always a good trait in a coworker. If he respects you, and this is the key, he is a tireless worker and will help you to the top by dragging you or pushing you along with him. But, a Capricorn first must hold you in high esteem and feel you are deserving of such assistance. Otherwise, he won't even bother to concern himself with you.

Capricorn stays home weekends. He holes up in his room to recharge his batteries. He draws the drapes and takes a vow of silence. He needs downtime and will take it when necessary. This means, he is off-limits socially during these times. In this light he can be viewed as aloof, antisocial, and reclusive. On occasion he is. Still, this is his work style, and he has two speeds, on or off.

Capricorn is a reader and can devour books. A collector, he loves antiques, vintage cars, or heirloom jewelry. He is a fan of the History Channel like his astrological opposite Cancer. He loves to give gifts to his friends and family and is often found shopping for or with his mom.

It is a rare Capricorn that does not hold a special place in his heart for his mother. Never forget, he has shared his dreams with her since he was young. It you want to get to know him, get to know his mom.

Sometimes the greatest joy for the Capricorn is to share his success with his mother. If you want to motivate Capricorn, mention a perk for mom. Case in point, Elvis said of his purchase of a home for his mother, "It's something my mother always wanted but never talked about. It was as if she didn't want to let anyone know about her dreams. But I knew. I wanted to get my mama a home."

The Capricorn cure for a morale problem is to butt his head against authority and demand changes. Never one to acquiesce, he is ready for a showdown. Born with a strong identity, he will state his mind and opinions and take his chances on the pink slip.

Capricorn finds it difficult to work with people who oppose him. He can do it and will do it, however, until that mysterious timing of his tells him otherwise. If he is forced to concede in any endeavor, look for his face to turn to stone. One look and even the steeliest opponent will back off.

It is his fervent will, his brave soul, that makes Capricorn the able leader. He can stifle a retort, hold back his true feelings, but will not abandon his dreams. And he will not deal with dishonesty, for he speaks what he thinks, which sometimes is unfortunate.

Although given to quiet, somber times, for the most part Capricorn is a "what you see is what you get" type of person. He worries and gets caught up in the negative from time to time, but never for long. After all, he has a mission and not even an off day deters him.

THE CAPRICORN LEARNING STYLE

Concrete Sequential ㆆ *Practical* ㆆ *Hands-On* ㆆ *Driven*

The way in which a Capricorn learns, or the way in which his mind works, is considered concrete when viewed in the context of the Gregorc Model of Learning Styles.

Everyone and every sign observe the same sights and sounds, yet each perceives them in different ways. While at some level we all see what we want to see, we still convert information in two distinct fashions. One perceptual quality is the concrete learning style.

When you think or perceive in a concrete way, you need to be organized, complete tasks, and feel you have value because you are productive. Capricorn schedules and plans in advance. He keeps receipts and time management studies, and he can find his car key, appointment book, and check register within seconds.

Capricorn asks questions, writes down instructions, and wants memos clarified. Once he has done this, however, he is quick to move on to other tasks. He is not as obsessive as the Virgo, but both pay attention to details. For example, the Capricorn wants you to tell him about your goals and expectations. He needs to hear it first. He wants to know your ideas, your plans, and then create an order around that knowledge.

The second component to learning has to do with how we order our information. The Capricorn prefers a straightforward method of learning, which is most often referred to as sequential learning. Capricorn has a special talent for seeing the practical side of things. He knows how to make things work and work for him. He plans and creates in a step-by-step manner, whether it is in office restructuring or his own career path.

Capricorn is neither vague nor veiled; he is specific. He wants detailed instruction because he wants to know that he is doing his job correctly. He works well with checklists and weekly reviews.

The learning style of the Capricorn is often punctuated with seeing things as more important than other people do and with a high degree of impatience. Everything is serious business with Capricorn.

THE BEST WAY FOR A CAPRICORN TO LEARN

Observation ♑ Using a Checklist

Capricorn prefers to solve problems one at a time right off the checklist. He likes instructions, not dictates.

Capricorn learns by observation and listening, using all his five senses. He notices who was successful and why. He listens to the way people communicate and learns how he needs to talk to them.

This is why so many Capricorns are talk show hosts and hostesses. Like the Gemini, Capricorn understands the power of speech.

For all his conservative, sequential tendencies, Capricorn is never afraid to take risks. I know of one who, during his downtime from acting, decided to start a rock band. He figured one branch of performing was the same as another and jumped right in.

Of course, by now you guessed it. He was a success. Capricorn almost always is.

While logical and sequential, Capricorn Martin Luther King Jr. trusted his faith in addition to hard data. He said, "Take the first step in faith. You don't have to see the whole staircase, just take the first step." Capricorn, born with destiny calling, takes that first step in faith, like Dolly Parton when she left the holler. Capricorn always trusts himself enough to initiate things.

The Capricorn profile includes his need to accomplish. He knows from his early days that he was born to do something special. He senses that he is somehow different, and this is both worrisome and a source of pride. Capricorn has a sense of fate.

Capricorn is the last of the earth signs. All the moneymaking, resourceful qualities of earth come together to create a public figure, someone who shows us all how to make the best of things.

Capricorn is the Forrest Gump of the zodiac. He overcomes all obstacles to be the man of the hour, or as in Elvis's case, the person of the century by popular vote for the *New York Times Magazine*.

THE CAPRICORN BOSS

Verbose ♑ Gives Second Chances

The Capricorn boss is often even more difficult to describe and classify than is the Capricorn employee. Just as Capricorn is different, one from the other, physically and mentally, Capricorn has his management quirks and peculiarities.

Capricorn can be verbose. When he gets to talking, he becomes more lively and, in fact, downright gabby. His striking powers in business, the ability to organize and work hard, will be the one common denominator.

When Capricorn writes policy, it is elaborate and scholarly. It will be backed by tradition, society, and customary thinking. No matter how conflicting his venues may seem, Capricorn always veers right back to the teachings of tradition and convention.

Capricorn usually comes into positions of authority in later life, around his late 50s. When most of his friends are thinking about retirement, Capricorn is finally getting his best opportunities and will keep working just to be able to make his dream a reality.

Of course, the younger Capricorn successes will note that their big career breaks came at the age of twenty-eight to thirty. Regardless of Capricorn's age, he will act older and more than a bit aloof. He is even considered something of a snob upon close reflection.

Unlike the Aries who waits for the first advance of the curve, Capricorn waits for the crest. He wants you to understand the timing of this. He also wants his employees to be up and running for any changes in the tides of fortune.

Capricorn cannot stand employees who take credit for something they have not actually done or, worse yet, take credit from someone. Any form of deceit is abhorrent to the Capricorn manager or supervisor.

Disloyalty is a trait that Capricorn cannot understand. He can understand convictions that do not agree with his or rebellions in spirit, but he will not forgive his employees any lack of devotion to his causes or projects.

One famous Capricorn boss, Thomas Watson Jr., was one of the few successes not born to a disadvantaged situation. However, his story is one, once again, of the goat having to do things his own way. His father was the president and founder of IBM. Watson Jr., riddled with self-doubts, feared he could not take over his father's corporation. Eventually, he not only took over, but surpassed his father's efforts.

The defining management style at IBM continues to be people-oriented. Watson Jr., who needed a few second chances in his youth himself, believes in the policy of giving an employee another chance to prove his worth. Who more than a Capricorn understands the diamond-in-the-rough theory?

Really, the Capricorn boss is good at being part dad. Remember this when he appears so unapproachable. Like his ruler, grandfather time, Capricorn can be counted on.

CAPRICORN SUCCESS STORIES

Elvis Presley was the American dream personified. Poverty stricken with not a chance in ten million to succeed, Elvis overcame all obstacles to become one of the most famous and beloved entertainers of the twentieth century.

Martin Luther King Jr. had a dream for America. His dream was to end racial segregation. He believed that "as individuals we have the moral right and responsibility to disobey unjust laws." This belief was outrageous enough to land him in jail.

A Capricorn will never shy away from anything he believes in. Not for the FCC, the FBI, or Caesar.

Cicero has become synonymous with the written word. He was considered one of Rome's greatest orators as well as a man of letters. Like many other Capricorns, he began his early career as a lawyer. He did not belong to the Roman aristocracy, which was difficult back in B.C. He had another problem; he refused to make peace with Caesar. Capricorn always has a problem with authority figures.

Cicero's writings, for which he was renowned, were rich prose styles. His dialogues were rich in history. His treatises were appreciated for their gentlemanly, genial tone, even when his face had turned to stone.

So, Stern, Schlessinger, and Limbaugh were not the first to have sway with words. Even David Letterman, an Aries with his moon in Capricorn, adds to the contemporary commentary with his top-ten list. Somehow, Capricorn wants to have his say and the last word on just about everything.

Albert Schweitzer's legacy was not just that he was a master theologian and a revered doctor and missionary. His great legacy may well be his insight that without a "reverence for life" modern civilization will decay. Schweitzer has spoken; are you listening?

Famous Capricorns overcome, and they leave us with something beyond themselves. This is their gift. Capricorns teach us it is not where you start that counts but where you end up. This is their lesson.

♑

OTHER FAMOUS CAPRICORNS

David Bowie	Cuba Gooding Jr.
Louis Braille	Val Kilmer
Jim Carrey	Susan Lucci
Frank Doubleday	Ricky Martin
Mel Gibson	Tolstoy

RESOURCES

Coffey, Frank. 1997. *The Complete Idiot's Guide to Elvis*. New York: Alpha Books.

Miner, Margaret, and Hugh Rawson. 1994. *The International Dictionary of Quotations*. New York: Signet Books.

Pritchett, Price. 1994. *New Work Habits for a Radically Changing World*. Dallas, TX: Prichett & Associates.

CHAPTER 11

THE HUMANITARIAN

AQUARIUS ▪ JANUARY 20 TO FEBRUARY 19

HOW TO SPOT AN AQUARIUS

Highly Individualistic 〰 *Analytical* 〰 *Absentminded*

Aquarius wanders around halls and corridors distracted and adorable. Polarized by magnetic forces of life the rest of us are not tuned in to, he looks around, and up, and forgets to keep his feet firmly planted. Here you find the pigeon-toed, slightly staggering, choppy, or sudden movements in walk that are as unique as the Aquarius himself.

Every Aquarius has the hint of the absentminded professor, bumbling his way about, good-hearted and eccentric. Each one walks with his head in the clouds, thinking no doubt of some important discovery or building Utopia.

The nobility of profile, found in Michael Jordan, Tom Selleck, and Lisa Marie Presley, suggests the highly individualized one-of-a-kind persona that is most telling about Aquarius.

Yes, he is different. You know this from the start. He cares about you, and he cares about humanity. He believes that one person can make a difference. His life will show you that. So will his career.

One of Aquarius's most notable characteristics is that he analyzes everything. When presented with his contract and personnel guidelines, he can't help himself. He needs to examine it, with a curious detachment and that faraway look in his eyes. You would swear he wouldn't remember a thing he read. Instead, he has questions. He ponders why paragraph C came before paragraph G. He may be too polite to ask at the start, but he'll get to it eventually.

Aquarius often ends up in careers that are out of the ordinary, like his attire. He is the scientist, astronomer, astrologer, astronaut, computer whiz, lighting specialist, electrician, scientific photographer, or the beloved local weatherperson.

The typical Aquarius is not a leader; he is the example. He has his own standard of excellence, and it is impressive. Whatever he undertakes, he does it with his whole heart, to follow his bliss and nourish his soul.

Being a standard of excellence himself, it is interesting to note what Michael Jordan says about this: "You have to expect things of yourself before you can do them."

Aquarius has been setting principles for the rest of us since the beginning of time. Aquarius has dreams of furthering mankind in intellectual pursuits of one sort or the other. While highly individual, he is the humanitarian and wants his work to promote a better world. It is rare to find an Aquarius who has not or is not doing some volunteer or community service.

WHAT DRIVES THE AQUARIUS?

The Future ~~~ *The Need to Do Something Different*

The future drives the Aquarius. He sees the gold medal, the championship, the syndication, the invention, the tomorrows, while the rest of us get stuck in today. Aquarius hockey great Wayne Gretzky gives a nod to the future in his statement, "I skate to where the puck is going to be, not where it is."

Aquarius knows that the mind is the source of all that you create in your life, whether it is spiritually or materially. The Aquarian mind is the source of his creativity and dreams. No matter what he does, he is driven by his intellect as well as his special relationship with the anticipated. Aquarius is not driven by the need to acquire or have power over things. He just wants to do something different and enjoy himself doing it.

Aquarius has a special knack for inventing. Famous Aquarius inventions have been the television, Xerox machines, the typewriter, electricity—all coincidentally considered astrologically ruled by the sign of Aquarius.

The earth signs Taurus, Virgo, and Capricorn assist Aquarius in his work by helping him make money from his unique abilities. Or, in the case of Virgo and Capricorn, earth can work alongside Aquarius with dedication and stamina.

Fellow air signs of Gemini and Libra understand what others would consider the impossible flights of fancy that Aquarius takes from time to time. But, unlike Libra and Gemini, Aquarius wants to investigate what has been done and what can be done better. Of the three signs, Aquarius is more inclined toward tedious fact-finding to support his theories.

Fire signs Aries, Leo, and Sagittarius can promote the Aquarian's inventions and discoveries. Aries helps Aquarius put his remarkable ideas on paper, Leo sends the press releases, and Sagittarius takes it global. Remember, Aquarius works well with just about everyone, for he was born under the sign of friendship.

Water signs Cancer, Scorpio, and Pisces seem to bring emotion into the often just-a-tad-detached Aquarius life. Aquarius has no initial thought of the profits of his work, so Cancer can sell it, and Scorpio can give Aquarius the passion to devote himself to his dream. Pisces adds another dimension entirely to the Aquarian works, for Pisces is often at the Patent Office moments before Aquarius remembers the address.

It happens in this Universe that similar ideas come to several people at the same time. During Aquarian Thomas Edison's life-time, Pisces Alexander Graham Bell's inventions preceded or coin-cided with Edison's. In many ways, one helps the other with the missing part of their discovery. They don't even need to know one another to do this.

THE AQUARIUS WORK STYLE

Works in Spurts
Needs a Little Extra Time to Do Things to His Satisfaction

Aquarius likes to work in interesting, exciting, and odd offices. You know the end office with no windows? The one with the strange plaids and patterns mixed together that no one else wants? It would be perfect for Aquarius. He likes to mingle and wander, and he understands a room that provides stimulation and things to be perplexed by.

Aquarius, while able to work on the same project for seemingly forever, likes to work in spurts. He is happy working on the floor or on long tables. He wants to be comfortable so he can concentrate. As you've gathered by now, your idea of comfort may not be the same as his.

His environment must be flexible, can be distracting. He may actually work better with a little noise or music. Aquarius does not like to be completely alone.

Aquarius, who tends to need stimulation, works better if his hours allow for flexibility. You can expect the unexpected with Aquarius, and while he may show up at 6 A.M. for years, one day he may become a night owl and want to start his work later in the day.

When given assignments, he might ask for extensions or need a little more time to finish. His mind has not necessarily been wandering; he would just rather not do a task than not do it to his satisfaction.

And, one more thing—don't expect him to get emotional over every idea that comes his way. He will keep his emotions in check. His work style is a quietly self-possessed one.

THE AQUARIUS STRENGTHS

Logical-Mathematical Intelligence ≋ *A Good Problem Solver*
A Good Decision Maker

While many different kinds of intelligence exist, each astrological sign possesses one or more areas in which he is most likely to excel. Aquarius functions best at the logical, mathematical level.

People who are gifted in the areas of mathematical and logical intelligence usually are the same people who are great scientists and inventors.

Aquarius uses these skills in ways other than the actual work of finances or figures. Aquarius is a good decision maker. He is able to solve problems whether work related or not.

Much of the Aquarius ability to solve the mysteries of the universe in a scientific fashion, or understand how a fax really works, is related to logic. This same logic can be applied to any business decision.

The Aquarius may make the simple deduction that he will be a better ballplayer if he practices a half hour extra every day. Or that he can, after seventy-six prior attempts to invent a typewriter that really works, come up with one upon which all other models are based.

Christopher Sholes, who invented the typewriter, solved some of the earlier problems with the keyboard layout by adding a shift key for upper- and lowercase letters. Aquarius can logically figure out the way to create a better product. He excels at building the proverbial better mousetrap.

Aquarius may not say much about his work, but he thinks about it a lot of the time.

THE AQUARIUS FAVORITE WORK ENVIRONMENT

Unexplored Paths ≋ *Positions That Offer Discovery*

Aquarius loves to use his enormous vision. He likes to wander in large crowds, so working for a large corporation suits him fine. Because he always has his own agenda, he often appears to be set apart from the crowd in some way or another. His skill is in unifying rather than blending.

The favorite path for Aquarius is the unbeaten one. President Abraham Lincoln said it best when he acknowledged, "Towering genius disdains a beaten path. It seeks regions hitherto unexplored."

Aquarius loves to go where no one else has gone before. Better yet, he loves to do things in a way that has not been done before. This is how he prefers to work. The unexplored and the unexpected characterize his favorite work arena. Life is full of changes for Aquarius. Why should his work environment be any different?

THE AQUARIUS EMPLOYEE/COWORKER

An Optimist ~~~ *Sincere* ~~~ *Good at Experimentation*

As an employee, Aquarius stands out from the rest. One reason is that he is exceptionally kind. He is extraordinarily thoughtful of his fellow associates. In a run-you-down, run-you-over kind of world, Aquarius is a gift. Sure, now and then there will always be an exception but an exception it is.

Aquarius hardly notices friction at work. When he hears of this, he raises his voice a pitch in wonder. "Really? Why for heaven's sake, such and so is so nice, and this is such a great place to work." Others may want to take Aquarius to task for not being aware, or failing to see the negative. But, alas, it is pointless. Aquarius sees mostly the good.

Aquarius is ahead of his time. He does not factor in race or creed. He is oblivious to the privileges of money or fame. He sees equality in every man.

Aquarius is not a pat-you-on-the-back, glad-handing, let's-do-lunch kind of person. He is sincere. When you are his friend, you are his friend 100 percent. When you are not, for whatever reason, he will be pleasantly aloof. Never unkind, just unavailable.

Ruled by higher vibrations, it should not surprise you that your Aquarius coworker can pick up on your feelings and intentions as if by radar. So, if you have any unscrupulous plots or double-dealing going on at work, don't participate within any distance of the Aquarius-born. Aquarius cannot read your mind like some of the water signs, but he has built-in antenna for the shady or underhanded.

Aquarius is agreeable with almost any work plan or proposal. He can also take a lot of criticism, but never think he does not have his limits. He does. Push past and you will see him become the foreboding dark cloud. He will be done with you or the situation after that.

When there is tension and discord at work, the Aquarius will go for a walk, take some time off to go to the planetarium, repair something, reread manuals, meditate, or get to a yoga class—in an effort to separate himself from tension. A few, such as Ronald Reagan, wander off and take a nap.

An inner spark drives the Aquarius. He comes into this world with his own agenda. Thomas Edison was eccentric enough that he did not know that he accomplished the impossible when he created his 1,000 inventions with only a trace of education and an abundance of experimentation and focus.

Remember, Michael Jordan did not make the high school basketball team. It was later that he developed such focus.

Never say never with the Aquarius associate.

THE AQUARIUS LEARNING STYLE

Needs a Chance to Deliberate ≋ *Takes His Time to Gather All of the Data*

The way an Aquarius learns or the way in which his mind works is considered abstract when viewed in the context of the Gregorc Model of Learning Styles.

Everyone and every sign observes the same sights and sounds, yet each perceives them in different ways. While at some level we all see what we want to see, we still convert information in two distinct fashions. One perceptual quality is abstract intelligence.

The abstract thinker possesses a certain depth of insight. While Aquarius appears to be perpetually in another world, or his thoughts far, far away, he is in fact quite an analytical person. He normally has a high intellect, a certain precision of knowledge.

One negative quality of people who lose themselves in thought is that they appear to be a little out of touch with the real world. Imagine for a moment what others thought of Edison with his limited education, tackling the realm of electricity. Or for that matter, remember the controversy over Darwin's theory?

Aquarius learns by experimentation. He uses logic and reason. He perceives things in numbers. He keeps things, issues or data, factual. But, the biggest plus of all is that he has the ability to change. He may be stubborn, but he will make appropriate changes.

Aquarian Darwin believed that it is not the strongest, or the most intelligent who survive, but the species or person that is the most responsive to change. In this regard, Aquarius is a survivor.

If you want to sell an idea or product to Aquarius, present data, numbers, and a full explanation. Give him material to read. He will actually read it. Most importantly, give him time to make a decision.

Aquarius thinks in the minority, since there are many more concrete thinkers than there are those who think largely in the abstract. He can disturb some concrete thinkers who want to make leaps in logic, see the entire forest and beyond before even knowing what trees are planted there. So give Aquarius a break. His ideas are often unpopular and nearly always light-years ahead of his peers.

The second component to learning is how we order our information. Aquarius prefers to do things in a uniform way. His preferences are to analyze, find structure and logic, be objective and deliberate. He feels more comfortable with a system or sequence to his work organization. He prefers a sequential process to his information.

One of the common themes of a successful company and a company success, which the Aquarius can be, is the use of first names, management by wandering around, and a certain genuine informality.

In the book *In Search of Excellence*, the authors found that the most effective managers, supervisors, and leaders were superior at abstraction as well as the most mundane of details. This accurately describes the Aquarius way of thinking.

THE AQUARIUS INTELLIGENCE

Logical-Mathematical ~~~ *Shows Up Well on IQ Tests*

Howard Gardner, Harvard professor and prominent researcher, has developed the theory that there are many different kinds of intelligence. He has identified seven while others are speculative.

The Aquarius type of intelligence is logical-mathematical, and he usually does well on traditional math and IQ tests. People with this skill see things in a logical fashion, in numbers and patterns. Not easily overwhelmed, they can break down a problem or idea into manageable segments. They are intelligent beyond the norm.

This ability gives Aquarius the chance to succeed in many occupations. With the ability to "break it down," nothing is overwhelming or impossible. Aquarius can follow his passions in a logical fashion. Whether or not Aquarius chooses a career in finance or numbers, he can use his gift to become many diverse types of professional.

Did Oprah stop at being a weatherperson? Did Garth Brooks remain strictly a country singer? Both actually parlayed their talents into many other facets of their lives.

For example, Aquarius can practice his sport an extra two hours a day to really define his ability. Or the Aquarius artist knows how many portions of the canvas must be covered in a determined amount of time to finish the commission. Part of any success, after all, is determination and follow-through.

The Aquarius was born for the Internet Age. He finds surfing a natural way of meeting new friends and expanding his neighborhood.

Aquarius understands the value of networking; he knows there is power in organizations. He perceives that knowledge is power. It may appear haphazard with Aquarius, but he understands the principles of persuasion. He takes networking, knowledge, and his love of people and, like the alchemist, turns them into his personal gold.

THE AQUARIUS BOSS

Is Futuristic ≋ *Is Distant* ≋ *May Have Unpopular Opinions*

You've heard the term *Honest Abe*? It comes from a reference made about Abraham Lincoln. He had some revolutionary ideas, not all of which were well received to say the least. But, he came from an honest place. He said what he meant and that was that. It is much the same for the supervisor born under the sign of Aquarius.

Aquarius would rather find a few honorable, truthful persons to work with him than large numbers. He surrounds himself with those who share his ethics and principles.

Aquarius really didn't plan on being your boss. He probably would prefer to be a consultant or working in his peculiar office on some rocket fuel solution or some homeless shelter benefit. Nonetheless, he is there—rather indifferently it may appear, but not so.

Your Aquarius boss is committed to whatever task is at hand. If a fellow January/February–born boss were quoted as saying, "Genius is 1 percent inspiration and 99 percent perspiration," imagine what yours is going to expect from you. He will want hard work and lots of it. He won't be demanding about it; he won't even appear to notice what you've been up to. But, please, if you want job security, do your best. Don't slack off because the manager seems preoccupied.

The Aquarius boss will need backing every now and again from his employees when he comes up with some plan or idea that is years ahead of its time. A dear, pigeon-toed, absentminded Aquarius friend of mine, a minister, found himself without favor and losing his job over the idea that it was perfectly all right to allow blacks in the South to become church members in the 1950s.

As unthinkable as the idea that blacks should not be members of a church is to us today, so was his idea on the meaning of Christianity in the '50s—that everyone was welcome in his church.

No one backed him, and he left the ministry. So when you see Aquarius come up with new ideas and thoughts, and new ways to make the world a better place, please assist him. He would do the same for you.

Think of poor Darwin; his theories of natural selection were doubted for fifty to eighty years. So be prepared for some doubters and naysayers around your futuristic boss. Setting examples in the workforce is a hard thing to do.

AQUARIUS SUCCESS STORIES

Two words: Michael Jordan.

Then, of course, there is Oprah Winfrey. Talk about setting examples and trying to build a utopia.

Elizabeth Blackwell, the first woman to receive a medical degree in the United States, was very unpopular. Doctors refused to work with her or did so reluctantly and with hostility. They just did not want to admit a woman into their doctoring circle.

Blackwell started medical school in 1848 after a series of schools rejected her application. Since no institution would hire her, she was unable to practice medicine. Then no one would rent office space to her.

Finally, in Aquarius-like fashion she bought a home and opened her office. Eleven years after starting school her name was listed on the medical register of the United Kingdom. She was the first woman doctor listed there.

Who else but an Aquarius would become the father of science fiction, Jules Verne? Try to picture a nineteenth-century writer forecasting so many of the twentieth-century discoveries. His science contained little fiction. So far ahead of others with his Aquarius thinking and his visions, Verne foresaw the ability for space travel, submarines, and even motion pictures.

One cannot mention Aquarius difficulties without the tribulations and actual trial of Galileo, the famous Italian mathematician, astronomer, and physicist. He actually laid many of the foundations for scientific experiments. Let me start with a list of his Aquarius traits:

1. He was able to time the oscillations of a swinging lamp from the beat of his pulse. A little off the wall, but terribly good logic and verifiably correct.
2. He waited three years to disclose his findings about the solar system and the sun being the center of it. No point rushing headlong into opposition.
3. He was summoned to Rome and tried by the Inquisition. Here he was forced to declare all his beliefs and writings to be false. He had to declare that he was mistaken in his discovery that the earth revolved around the sun. Not everyone reacts favorably to change and new ideas or facts. Once again, the Aquarius was swimming against the currents.

4. Unable to tell a lie, he got up from his knees and shouted "Nonetheless, it does move" (around the sun). So much for changing the Aquarius's mind.

We all need to listen a bit more to our curious Aquarius friends and bless them in their journeys. They are our futures.

≋

OTHER FAMOUS AQUARIANS

Jennifer Aniston	Jane Seymour
Christie Brinkley	George Stephanopoulos
Sheryl Crow	John Travolta
Mia Farrow	Eddie Van Halen
Ted Koppel	Alice Walker
Paul Newman	Vanna White
Greg Norman	

RESOURCES

Bridgewater, William, and Seymour Kirtz, eds. 1963. *The Illustrated Columbia Encyclopedia*. New York: Columbia University Press.

Miner, Margaret, and Hugh Rawson. 1994. *The New International Dictionary of Quotations*. New York: Signet Books.

Tobias, Cynthia Ulrich. 1995. *The Way We Work*. New York: Broadman and Holman Publishers.

CHAPTER 12

THE RESEARCHER

PISCES ▪ FEBRUARY 19 TO MARCH 21

HOW TO SPOT A PISCES

Complex ✕ Sensitive ✕ Impressionable

Like the eleven other signs, Pisces is distinguishable by his walk, which is light, dancing, as if he has one foot underwater, feeling the river stones as he moves along just as his ruler the fish does.

Then there is the matter of the Pisces eyes, as mysterious and beautiful as the seas. Whether large and glistening brown, violet, ocean green, or twinkling blue, the eyes of the fish are one of Pisces' most striking features.

Pisces sees with more than his eyes, however. His sight goes straight to the heart of the universe, where he ponders the invisible forces of nature.

Compared to more ethereal matters, weaving his way around commerce and trade is child's play. While the rest of us muddle with five senses, he taps into his sixth sense effortlessly. This, then, is the potential of Pisces and the possibility to do the extraordinary.

Pisces is a daydreamer. He is imaginative. Give him the personnel guidelines and he may decide to make note of all the rhyming words. Or he may simply put his hands on it to feel its vibrations and decide whether this job, this place, these directions are a fit for him. So much of Pisces is vague, impractical, and fueled by moonbeams.

One of Pisces' most notable characteristics is his ability to intuit, to see through and beyond. His love of mystery and his dreams of the impossible set him apart from the rest of us. Man of the century Albert Einstein said, "The most beautiful thing you can experience is the mysterious."

Many times Pisces is in this world, but not completely a part of it. There is a fragment of Pisces that no one can understand, comprehend, or unravel. He will never bother to tell you that special part of himself either.

Pisces is complex, and you can't quite tell what is going on behind his dreamy eyes. He is not interested in leading causes or people. He prefers to work alone. Pisces does such a stellar job at work that he is often promoted to positions of supervision. He is not usually happy in management, and when stress and discontent begin to take their toll, Pisces may prefer to take his former position back.

You see, Pisces cannot stand a lot of distractions and conflict. Too much stimulation or too little (a Pisces' system is finely tuned) and he can be something of a hypochondriac. Sometimes a real disease occurs, but even when it does not, Pisces will retreat into a world of fatigue.

For the most part, Pisces does not speak his mind. He may talk a lot but not really reveal his actual feelings about a matter. But every now and then, like a little solar flare, he erupts. Needless to say, you will be stunned. So much had been pent up emotionally. Personally, I would rather be near Mount Saint Helens at these times than a hurt or angered Pisces.

Which brings us to the dilemma that Pisces faces. What in the world do you say after you've said it all? The kind Pisces, who believes that old saying about sticks and stones, never wants to hurt anyone. Maybe it was a sugar high or a reaction to MSG. Maybe, the wine. Pisces cannot believe that his eruption was from somewhere deep inside him.

Pisces often ends up in careers in research or chemistry, as an underwater explorer, a private investigator, pharmacist, hospital employee, model, or poet. Anything is possible, because with Pisces anything is possible.

Pisces has lived a life involved in the spiritual, the care of the soul and nurturing of others since the beginning of time. Pisces is attracted to the metaphysical or any field sparked by the imaginative process. He has been the missionary, the troubadour, and the caretaker, and usually Pisces has more than one major career change within his lifetime.

Whatever his career may be, he can, given the right set of circumstances, be inspired.

WHAT DRIVES THE PISCES?

His Inner Voice Ӿ *Ancient Wisdoms*

Something in the Pisces' soul must be stirred to drive him to accomplish anything. If he has not heard his inner voice speak of his destiny, or even murmur about the position advertised, he will take no initiative.

Pisces lives with one foot in another world. He was born with a star in his palm, under a magical and portentous sky.

When Pisces talks of motivation, he only understands it in terms of stirring. Something awakens in him one starry night:

perhaps a gypsy whisper. Who knows how Pisces connects to his personal destiny? But I believe the Pisces' sense of wonder is what unites him to his personal wisdom. Pisces is often wise.

Pisces understands the air signs because, like him, their feet do not often touch the ground. Pisces can think out of the box like Gemini, Libra, and Aquarius. Einstein thought as far as to relative time and space, for heaven's sake. Many times Pisces has a better grasp on eternity than tomorrow. As a creative team, the air signs and Pisces can surmount the naturally creative Leo.

Fire signs Aries, Leo, and Sagittarius like spark, pop, and dazzle, which only annoys Pisces' nervous system. He feels frayed and more than a little singed by contact. After the initial startling proximity to all that energy, Pisces finds the fire signs all have something unique to offer him. Aries can talk him through fears because Aries knows so few. Leo can promote Pisces with people of influence who the Pisces would never encounter otherwise. Sagittarius can take Pisces for an excursion right here on earth and open the Pisces' mind to the here and now of any project.

Earth signs Taurus, Virgo, and Capricorn work well with Pisces. Taurus, inspired by bohemians and the unknown, helps Pisces think in more concrete terms. Virgo, so opposite Pisces, is like a mirror reflection in many ways, which can be beneficial in business. Capricorn attracts Pisces because an innate understanding of dreams with the Capricorn creates an instant bond. Here is mutual support, and Pisces senses it right away.

Fellow water signs Cancer and Scorpio are wonderful teammates for Pisces. Ah, but it is Scorpio who gets the sometimes uninspired, lackluster Pisces to listen for that inner voice. Pisces needs to feel the passion for a vision, as dreams alone are not enough.

Pisces gets along well with anyone really because he is a chameleon of sorts.

THE PISCES WORK STYLE

Needs Acknowledgement)(*Is Sensitive*)(*Does Not Like to Be Rushed*

Ever worked around someone who worked in fits and starts? Pisces can be the most meticulous, detailed person and then go for months unable to find his office keys, let alone the office.

It won't surprise you then to know he will not be 100 percent consistent about decor either. You most likely will find ocean green and sea blue near him. A seascape on the wall, perhaps. Pisces usually will have a seashell somewhere in his environment. There is a reason for this.

Symbolic, the seashell reminds Pisces that things are not always as they seem. The sound of the ocean can be heard in the shell. In addition it is a reminder that the desert itself was once his beloved sea. There is a certain mystery in that, which appeals to Pisces' senses.

Other items Pisces is attracted to and often surrounded by are amethyst rocks and small tin (his lucky metal) accessories. Sometimes a trinket from the past, perhaps copies of some long ago Parisian flea market knickknack clutter his work space. Finally, look for scattered gifts from coworkers who clearly are enmeshed in Pisces' life, for he is loveable and people come bearing gifts.

Throwing new assignments his way won't work for Pisces. Take your time, approach him slowly, and put things in neat little piles. His mind may be opaque, nebulous even, to the rest of us, but you had better be clear to him.

While Pisces can read your mind, he needs to see you centered, focused, and quiet for a moment to set his eyes on you, to fix his gaze. He will tune in and then, once you get his attention, do a terrific job. He will do this because he wants to please you. Besides he wants to feel part of a family at work; please don't make him feel you are in his office only to deliver an assignment or instructions. You might injure his feelings.

If you want Pisces' attention, acknowledge him. Take your time to give instructions and become part of his day. While he works well in solitude, he does not want to feel isolated. There is a difference.

THE PISCES STRENGTHS

Intrapersonal Intelligence)(*An Innate Understanding of Situations*

While many different kinds of intelligence exist, each astrological sign possesses one or more areas in which he is most likely to excel. The Pisces is able to work alone and enjoys time to reflect, meditate, and come to conclusions in his own time. Because of this, Pisces is considered to possess an intrapersonal intelligence, which does not always respond to traditional testing for IQ as well as others. Einstein got off to a slow start in school, perhaps in part because of his strong intrapersonal mentality.

This form of IQ has a certain element of innate understanding. Because of this, Pisces is able to determine his own goals and aspirations without caving in to peer pressure. Sometimes the pondering nature of Pisces is mistaken for disinterest, or a certain slowness, but Pisces evaluates and looks for potential. Often the intrapersonal mentality does not share information until someone asks. Because Pisces is not boastful, is often quiet, and keeps to himself, he may be misconstrued. Pisces can be viewed with negative connotations until you discover some of his "weaknesses" are, in reality, strengths. He was not being shy or retreating, but he was working on some new insight or discovery.

There is something to be said for the silence of Pisces, as Mother Teresa, a Virgo and mirror opposite of Pisces, said, "God is the friend of silence. Trees, flowers, and grass grow in silence. See the stars, moon, and sun, how they move in silence." Often, when Pisces is silent, others think of this in negative terms. Yet, just beneath the surface, there is growth in Pisces' quiet. Silence allows him to do his research and free his intelligence.

THE PISCES FAVORITE WORK ENVIRONMENT

Quiet Ж *Environments Where He Can Help Others*

Pisces likes research labs, chemistry labs, photographic darkrooms, and places where the curious mixing of elements brings out the alchemist in him. Pisces likes the opportunity to make a difference in this world and is drawn almost like magic to hospitals, institutions, places that offer rehabilitation and healing. Retreats, gardens, temples, yoga centers have a certain lure for Pisces, as well.

Pisces can be found researching DNA, working with laboratory flasks and test tubes. Pisces crusades for new vaccines, volunteering at whatever cause tugs at his heart. Most often, Pisces is found near monasteries, temples, or churches, if only for a respite from a world in need of a little spiritual enlightenment.

Pisces has a natural love of silence; it helps him turn toward the pursuit of higher things, spiritual and emotional matters.

Aries started off the zodiac craving excitement and activity. Esoteric Pisces closes the zodiac contemplating inner peace and outer realms.

THE PISCES EMPLOYEE/COWORKER

Caring Ж *Funny* Ж *Artistic* Ж *Secretive*

Mix the mystical and the imaginative and you get Pisces. In other words, M + I = P. When you work with Pisces, he may surprise you by his near obsession with health, fears, and anxiety.

At first he may not let you in on his worries, but they will eventually surface. Or you may simply begin to notice his habits, which will be revealing. For instance, he may drive to an unknown office location three days ahead of his appointment, just to be sure he will not get lost or be late for his upcoming visit there.

You may overhear Pisces talk of packing for his company training. "I made a list on the computer last night of all the things I need to take and will keep working on it until I think I haven't left anything out that I need to bring with me." Pisces takes careful precautions because anything could go wrong at work.

You may notice the checking and double-checking of all memos and instructions that pass his desk. Another clue as to your Pisces coworker is that he will try to protect you and care for you and your fears. Pisces is compassionate.

The important thing is that Pisces will give you indications, rather than information. He is secretive by nature. Pisces is comfortable with the familiar but can see past it and is something of a seer about what the future holds for his company and yours. However, he may never share this with you. Why should he? Genius is not always well received.

On the weekend Pisces spends time alone or with a select few. Movies, music, arts, and painting take up his leisure time. Pisces often has an avocation or a talent totally unrelated to his work.

The remarkably witty and fun Pisces has a wonderful sense of humor. His cure for a morale problem is: 1) stay out of it or deny it, 2) bring homemade chocolate chip cookies, or 3) deliver a monologue on some unrelated subject.

If the problem gets too severe, if denial no longer works, he will move on. He is a caring, loving, terrific pal. His greatest harm is to himself.

THE PISCES LEARNING STYLE

Is Fueled by Change)(*Does Not Like Restrictions*

The way a Pisces learns or the way in which his mind works is considered abstract when viewed in the context of the Gregorc Model of Learning Styles.

Everyone and every sign observe the same sights and sounds, yet each perceives them in different ways. While at some level we all see what we want to see, we still convert information in two distinct fashions. While we use both, we have a preference. One perceptual quality is abstract intelligence.

When you think or perceive in an abstract way, you have the ability to believe what you cannot actually see. You appreciate the importance of imagination. Einstein said that he depended on the "free intuitive capacity of the human mind" in his work.

Management has recently acknowledged intuitive management style and has come to the realization that flexibility is a key in today's rapidly changing work environment.

The abstract thinker picks up on clues that others miss, both verbal and nonverbal. As a result of years of abstract thinking, the abstract thinker finds that his people skills improve over the years. His intuition also seems to improve over time.

Placing people above things and realizing that there is more to life than just the facts, the abstract thinker often excels in fields of discovery or service. For example, Pisces will tune you out if your report does not appeal to some quixotic process. Lines and columns of figures alone will not inspire him. He needs to make creative leaps into a theory, a piece of art, or a solution to a mystery.

Pisces wants to make a difference in the world. Tying him down to rigid rules and coloring between the lines is just not, well, romantic enough for him.

When making a presentation to Pisces, remember, like Michelangelo, he wants to be inspired, because when he is, he creates masterpieces.

THE PISCES INTELLIGENCE

Intrapersonal IQ)(*Random Learning Style*

Howard Gardner, Harvard professor and prominent researcher, developed the theory that many different kinds of intelligence exist. He has identified seven, while others are speculative.

Recently, emotional intelligence has been suggested as another form of IQ. Daniel Goleman's work on this has opened our eyes to the possibility of genius beyond more traditional measures. The importance of the varieties of mental capacities, or ways to be smart, may really reflect the passions that incline us toward our work.

Pisces, like his fellow water sign Scorpio, follows his heart when it becomes a passion. Pisces, however, thinks more randomly than does Scorpio.

While all of us process information from both a concrete and an abstract viewpoint, we have a preference. This preference is where we are most comfortable in learning and working situations.

If you want to work for or with a Pisces, remember he is an intrapersonal personality, with an abstract/random learning style. Pisces is also of the water element and the mutable mode astrologically. The mutable types are fueled by change. Pisces does not like a lot of restriction. While Pisces is not as enterprising as other signs, when he finds his desire he creates works that leave some of the greatest impressions on mankind. For Einstein, it was his theory of relativity; for the person across the way, it may be a new and exciting discovery just waiting its time.

THE PISCES BOSS

Double-Checks Everything)(*Has Uncanny Insights*

Pisces is not driven by the desire for power, so he does not gravitate toward jobs that are at the head of something. He can be promoted to that, but he normally ends up there by accident. Of course, there is no such thing as an accident, so this may be the result of some greater design than his own. Often, Pisces feels the hand of something bigger than him on his life's plan.

Pisces is talented in the arts, music, television, modeling, producing, where he can be brilliant. However, in less fanciful environments, Pisces is often a distracted boss.

Pisces may have worked for the company forever, mainly because he was concerned about making a job change and anxious about his monthly check. He did a good job, so why not accept the promotion? But, he did not in his heart of hearts desire it.

The Pisces boss fears authority to some degree and does not want to be in charge, unless he is running his own company or developing his own labs and hypotheses.

Pisces will check and double-check your work just as he does his own work. He will send out memos with plans A, B, and lots of Cs just in case.

His uncanny insights into you will startle you every now and then. Forget the "I think I feel a cold coming on" if you don't.

He will use these same insights to see your potential. Seeing potential and eventualities is his management genius.

Pisces hates to let go of a project for fear it might be wrong. This is where he needs to surround himself with people of good intent and few anxieties. Pisces needs to partner with warriors and those of more forceful natures.

Since Pisces is a dreamer, you need to dream a little with him. You may even find yourself a little codependent with your Pisces boss. He will have his own worries, sick days, hypochondria months, failed dreams, and emotional baggage. You will know a lot about these issues of his, but then again very little of the real substance of them.

Kaizen is the relentless quest for a better way, a higher ground in management. Pisces is naturally attracted to this philosophy, to the daily pursuit of doing things at the best level he can. When Pisces is doing what he desires, he works at this level.

Pisces, at his gold-dusted best, will keep you reaching for ways to express your personal highest self, to build the best product, write the best copy, or develop better customer relations. In this way, Pisces can build the ultimate competency level for the entire organization.

PISCES SUCCESS STORIES

On the first day of 2000, *Time* magazine selected Albert Einstein as the most important person of the twentieth century. The last of the zodiac signs, a Pisces, was the first of the picks.

Einstein was slow to talk, and later as an adult he did not drive. He described himself as a "dreamy and unorderly" child. By his twelfth year, he was teaching himself geometry; he mastered differential and integral calculus by sixteen.

Pondering the invisible forces of nature, Einstein believed in harmony in nature, stating, "the most incomprehensible thing about the world is that it is comprehensible." Along the way, in his Pisces lifetime, Einstein had a law named after him, as did another Pisces, Georg Ohm, who discovered the basic law of electric current flow.

Einstein worked from several areas of intelligence, as do other signs. However, like many Pisces, he was accomplished in many other areas. Einstein was a mathematician, musician, philosopher. Ultimately, it was his intrapersonal skills that led him to the horizons of the boundaries of the universe.

Einstein is said to have learned to connect with the universal mind. His favorite philosopher, Spinoza, believed that we can connect the eternity of the mind to the ability to intuit, and follower Einstein practiced it.

Einstein was a man of many incongruous and commonplace traits in the midst of his genius. He had a childlike curiosity about learning that never changed. Like countless other Pisces before and after him, he was vulnerable, an introvert, and happier with his own abstract thoughts than surrounded with people or things.

Children foretell their story early on as they take apart their cribs, publish their own newspapers, or express other unique talents. Einstein was no different in this respect. He was fascinated by magnets at the age of four or five, and this was his earliest work with gravity.

Einstein was a child, after all, playing with beads, stringing them together, matter and energy, space and time, watching the magnet for clues.

Michelangelo, another Pisces who gave us a masterpiece, lived as a sculptor, painter, architect, and poet. He spent four agonizing and clearly inspired years working on the Sistine Chapel. The religious and spiritual content is as artful as the mastery of the brush strokes. Like other Pisces, he sensed the hand of God in his life.

President James Madison was such a hypochondriac he went home to his father's estate where he thought he could study in peace and relative seclusion until he died. It was there he studied law and wound up in politics. From that, he inspired and drafted much of the Bill of Rights. Pisces eventually reaches out for his destiny and in doing that helps us with our own.

The author of "Nearer My God to Thee" was a poet and a Pisces. Pisces always finds a way to wind back to the religious, spiritual side of life. Remember that as he works in the lab, the darkroom, or his think tank or when he is struggling with his anxieties and fears in his early years and appears hopelessly disordered.

When all is said and done, the final signature on any evolved Pisces documents will be the mention of the creator.

)(

OTHER FAMOUS PISCES

Drew Barrymore
Alexander Graham
  Bell
Jon Bon Jovi
John Byron
Prince Edward of
  England
Kelsey Grammer
Henry Wadsworth
  Longfellow

Rupert Murdoch
Shaquille O'Neal
Linus Pauling
Aidan Quinn
Rembrandt
Renoir
Mickey Spillane
Sharon Stone
Ivana Trump

RESOURCES

Calder, Nigel. 1979. *Einstein's Universe*. New York: Greenwich House, Crown Publishers.

McEvoy, Frances. 1994. "Albert Einstein: Person of the 20th Century," *The American Federation of Astrologers*, Vol. 62, No.6.

Miner, Margaret, and Hugh Tawson. 1994. *The New International Dictionary of Quotations*. New York: Signet Books.

EPILOGUE

Back at the typical staff meeting we visited in the Introduction, the committee adjourns and joins the rest of the department for lunch.

Sweet-natured Donald is conversing with Molly and both are enjoying the discussion. Molly has great ideas for the organization and some interesting, almost peculiar suggestions on how things should be run. Donald appreciates her insights, but he thinks the more conservative proposals of Kay are good, too. Sometimes it is hard to decide just what should be implemented. Donald is ambitious, but not sure he wants to be a supervisor. Too many decisions make him uncomfortable.

Molly actually resists change at many levels, but you could never tell this by the way she runs her personal affairs. So many things have happened to her in her short life. Molly had hoped that she could stay in the department forever. The manager and Molly certainly get along well, even though Molly is an idealist and the manager an idea person.

Nick eats his veggie burger and listens to MaryAnn who has a stomachache. MaryAnn is worried about the new girl, Nan, who is so reticent—not exactly aloof, but, well, hesitant to join the others in many activities. Her nose is always in some research paper, her watery eyes glued to the computer. MaryAnn wonders if it's eye-strain or allergies or a private heartache that gives Nan the impression of near tears. MaryAnn vows to try to interact with Nan more.

Richard is impatient, as the waitress is too slow for his taste. He thinks all of this "sit and chat stuff" is a waste anyway. Maybe he could run around the block a few times after lunch to calm down. He notices the manager is talking about one of the several newspaper articles she had read this morning; "blah, blah, blah," he thinks.

Thomas quickly catches Richard's attention by asking about his client in a deep, throaty voice. As Kay speaks to the others, she notices Nick with his quiet manner. He's a workhorse, she thinks, as she continues on about the new format of *Bazaar* magazine. She tries to steer the conversation away from work.

The queen speaks and begins holding court. She talks about her upcoming trip to Italy, her recent encounter with a rock star, and how she just happens to know the partners of the possible merger. Everyone is fascinated.

Emma speaks up again about her concerns over the print campaign for her client. Serious as ever, Emma could be as determined as an old billy goat. The manager had heard how funny she was outside of work, but has never seen any evidence of it in the office. Still, everyone could count on Emma. She's as punctual as a clock, and more practical than necessary.

Emma's personal friend and coworker, Stella, is tall and thin, making the two of them look like cartoon characters when they're together. Actually, they're quite a team. Stella is ambitious like Emma but much less focused. She's sunny and fun, yet she has great aspirations. The manager sees something of herself in Stella.

Over lunch the manager has an opportunity to study the basic natures of her staff. Tonight she will read *Astrology on the Job* and hope for some further personality clues. Insights have never been one of her strengths, but perhaps she should try and be less super-ficial in her observations. Maybe in this way she can increase pro-ductivity and harmony.

Having read the book, can you now guess the astrological signs of each of our staff members?

The team you met in the Introduction:

- Neat Nick, a Virgo
- Kay, a Taurus
- The queen, a Leo
- MaryAnn, a Cancer
- The manager, a Gemini

The rest of the staff, from the Epilogue:

- Molly, an Aquarius
- Donald, a Libra
- Nan, a Pisces
- Richard, an Aries
- Thomas, a Scorpio
- Emma, a Capricorn
- Stella, a Sagittarius

And so it goes, at every gathering of coworkers, the twelve signs of the zodiac struggle for understanding and insight into the behaviors of the others.

Each of us is unique and has individual gifts of expression and talents to offer in the work arena. When you view your business relationships in light of the powers of the universe, your working world will take on a whole new meaning.

INDEX

Index